One Great Whole

One Great Whole

RYAN FULLMER UMARI

Copyright © 2010 by Ryan Umari

Revised Edition © 2024

All rights reserved. No part of this publication may be reproduced, stored in a retrieval system or transmitted, in any form, or by any means, electronic, mechanical, recorded, photocopied, or otherwise, without the prior permission of the copyright owner, except by a reviewer who may quote brief passages in a review.

Printed in the United States of America

ISBN: 978-0-578-67980-8

Contents

Acknowledgements 7

1: The Principle of Knowledge 11

2: The Principle of Identity 27

3: The Principle of the Whole 51

4: The Principle of Character 61

5: The Principle of Intelligence 73

6: The Principle of Worth 91

7: The Principle of Purpose 107

The Sequel: The Spirit of God 119

References 121

Acknowledgements

For their significant contribution to this series, I want to express my appreciation to a few people. First to Nyla, who lived the journey of taking these books from concept into reality- contributing to their shape along the way, and for years supporting the project emotionally, energetically, and spiritually. Thanks also to Jonathan Gullery and Vince Pannullo for their work on the layout and design of the books, and to Luis Peres, Sabartstudio, and my sister Tamara for their work on the illustration of the cover art of this first book. And a big thanks to Oxford Editing, and Zinah Mortensen for editing the books, and adding many of the chapter summary points you'll see along the way.

Also, a sincere thanks to everyone who read and gave feedback on the original version of One Great Whole. I want to give special thanks to Joey Baird and Brian Sabey for giving very detailed and helpful notes, and for being great friends. And to Drew for his humor and friendship over so many years. The first book has now been revised, the second and third books will be revised and released at some point in the future.

Thanks also to Paul and Bonnie Jean Thornley for years of

their loving influence on my life, and to my mom for doing a final read through of this book, and both my parents for their love and support throughout my life. And a huge thanks to my daughter Yana, who from the time we first learned she would be born, has been an incredible joy and inspiration in my life. You've grown into a person I respect, admire, and will always be proud of.

And although I hadn't met her before most of this was completed, I want to thank my wife Sarah for being the most caring, thoughtful, and supportive partner I could ever ask for. Thank you for supporting my passion for writing, and encouraging my effort to get these books into the world!

For this Earth

1

The Principle of Knowledge

INTRODUCTION: PUZZLE OF TRUTH

An interesting aspect of any law of physics or principle of mathematics is that its validity transcends human belief and understanding. Gravity, for example, does not cease to work upon an infant simply because she has not been taught about its effects. The universal principles of understanding, generally accepted by all people, provide a foundation of ideological harmony upon which the human collective can live and act in accord. No war has ever arisen between those who believe in the principles of addition and subtraction and those who do not. Furthermore, the application of principles of mathematics across all races and cultures serves as a unifying belief and practice that helps to bring human action and purpose into harmony.

As the famous precept declares that "a house divided

against itself cannot stand"[1], neither can a race of intelligent beings divided in purpose and priority maintain its power and dominion upon the earth. Ideological division and all aspects of subsequent societal conflict, the fruits of discordant purpose and action, threaten humanity. As ideological harmony or discord create either unified or divided priority or action, working to bring principles of divided understanding into the same degree of universal acceptance as principles of mathematics and other laws of the natural world provides a path toward greater societal peace and prosperity.

The greatest current ideological division that exists between human beings rests on the divide between science and religion, or between those who accept no principle of understanding unless it has been tested by the scientific method and those who believe and live their lives based on principles concerning intangible and often unverifiable realities. The progression of scientific understanding in the arenas of physics, chemistry, medicine, genetics, and many other disciplines, provide an expanding foundation from which to investigate religious and spiritual premises. There is unique opportunity to bring science and religion together in support of one another.

One Great Whole attempts to use the tools of logic and reason in conjunction with evidence related to unseen realities in order to harmonize ideological differences between Scientific and Religious communities. Parts of what might be called "the whole of perfect understanding" come from many different places. This work hopes only to bring together some of the major pieces and that others will continue, as many already are working, to try to harmonize discordant principles of human understanding into the great whole into which all truth and knowledge can be circumscribed. It is my hope that this attempt will help to decrease ideological discord among human beings and the actual discord that follows along these lines of conceptual division.

Each chapter seeks to bring spiritual premises, scientific research and logical deduction together in support of each other where possible. As each chapter builds off of premises established in previous sections, the book was designed to be read in order. This book was written in an effort to unite perspectives, ideologies, principles, and evidence already in existence, with a few new concepts, just as one might take a thousand puzzle pieces and find their relationship to each other, linking single pieces as well as sections in which many connections have already been made. Where the boundaries of the pieces may have seemed to be in conflict, with the slight turn of a piece in one direction or another, or with a link added in between, pieces can come together. Linking various pieces of truth can provide greater depth of understanding and in fact strengthen each individual principle. With a standard puzzle, the greater number of pieces that become linked allow for a greater vision of the whole; so too does piecing together principles of understanding begin to unfold a picture of the whole of existence, a picture of great beauty and purpose.

The thoughts presented are those stemming from the analytical reflection of the author and contributions of cited sources. This work stands independent of any institution or organization and any claims or errors are the singular responsibility of the author and no other entity or individual.

It is offered in respect to all those who give their time and resources to reading and pondering its message. As the author, I understand that choosing to give the time for such an endeavor, with all of the other demands life places, is a gift of the reader. It is my hope that you, the reader, receive as much from that investment of time in reading this book as I have received in writing it.

KNOWLEDGE AND POWER

As humans exist in a world where natural and physical laws exert their influence, the drive to obtain knowledge has been a quest to become less passive to forces that bear effect on life, such as disease, famine, and flood, and to have greater power in ensuring survival and other desired outcomes. Humans' awareness of many principles about the nature of the physical world have increased their safety within it.

Laws of physical and practical dynamics are some of the first principles that are taught to young children: "Don't touch the hot stove," "Look both ways before crossing the street," "Wash your hands before eating," "Don't stick your finger in the electric socket," "Be careful with sharp objects," and others. For adults, these principles have been understood for so long that at some point they began to be followed automatically, without any conscious thought. The common element to these rules is that they serve to protect people from forces that would cause potential harm if they did not live in obedience to them: the heat of the stove burner, the cars in the street, germs on our hands, electric shock, a sharp surface. All of these sources of harm exist and bear influence regardless of human understanding or awareness of them.

Where there is a dynamic that affects human beings, knowledge of it allows each person to alter his relationship to the law in operation from one of passivity to one of activity, or more control. For an example, take the situation of two people standing on a roof: the first understands the law of gravity, the second does not. The second decides to take a walk through the air to the next building and the force of gravity exerts its power on him even though he had no knowledge of it. His lack of understanding results in serious injury. The other also desires to go to the next building, but, understanding the law of gravity, he walks down the stairs and across the street to his destination. Both had the same desire, but one had more power to achieve this end because he more fully understood the dynamics in his world that needed to be negotiated.

For this reason, when a person evaluates experience and derives knowledge in the practical world and the world of human relationships, his purpose is the same as discerning knowledge of the physical world: to understand the nature of things in order to increase power over outcomes in categories of life that are personally important. These categories include financial security, personal health, nutrition, happiness, love, and others. The mind works to evaluate experience and organize its data into guiding principles. These guiding principles

> *Where there is a dynamic that affects human beings, knowledge of it allows each person to alter his relationship to the law in operation from one of passivity to one of activity, or more control.*

form the foundation of understanding from which one will live and act.

Rules are therefore made about every aspect of life, about anything and everything: "Don't tell jokes to Bob, he doesn't understand my sense of humor"; "Do put salt on eggs, it improves their taste"; "Don't kiss on the first date". These and other principles of understanding are the building materials used to construct personal reality.

Whether accurate or not, the principles of under-standing derived from cognitive determinations of experience transform an unknown and insecure world into one of greater perceived stability and security. Just as the flip of a light switch in a dark room illuminates the form and color of the objects within, so too do these conceptual determinations give form and definition to reality. For example, most people have not actually looked though a microscope and seen a virus or a sub-atomic particle, but through language, one can conceptually understand the nature, form, and substance of such realities. Indeed, the substance of personal reality, or our relationship to most objects and events in the world of experience, while initially derived from the senses, solidifies and resides in conceptual form. Even though cognitive determinations are formed from subjective experience, and many times based on less than accurate interpretations, they are the foundation of choice and action – they shape drive and purpose.

The principles of conceptual understanding which form the foundation of one's personal structure of reality arrive not only through personal experience and conceptual reflection, but also through reliance on other sources of information such as parents, schools, and television programs. Examples of descriptions of reality derived from personal experience might include statements such as "Math is hard", "Sarah is friendly", or "People think I'm funny". Examples of descriptions adopted from the experience of other sources might include statements of conventional wisdom, such as "The best security is a good education"; they may also include factual statements, such as "The earth revolves around the sun".

The positive aspect about relying on information about life from other sources is that one can receive a lot of understanding quickly, without deriving the conclusions themselves. There are many areas of knowledge such as geography, medicine, mathematics, or physics, that humans would simply know very little about without relying on the information derived and expanded over the course of hundreds or even thousands of years.

The difficulty with relying on the knowledge of other sources is that since one is not personally deriving this information, one must accept and act on the validity of these sources on some degree of uncertainty. Not all of the information that people receive from other sources is accurate. Parents, educators, media, and other sources give a mixture of fact, cultural tradition, superstition, good practical wisdom, strong probability, and absolute fiction. As one's conceptual understanding of the world is a primary influence of action, human action is a product of fact and fiction, knowledge and ignorance.

When a person makes interpretations of experience into definite rules by which to live, he creates limitations, as other possible interpretations must necessarily be excluded. Obeying the law of gravity excludes the possibility of jumping off of high things pretending to be Superman. The limitations are intended to exclude risks and dangers in order to protect and ensure things like survival and good health. Every time a person chooses to obey a law which pertains to actual dynamics at work, he is building a shelter – excluding actual danger without and protecting life within. Every time he chooses to live in obedience to a principle where the risk is an illusion or is exaggerated, he is building a prison rather than a shelter. The limitations confine his action without actual purpose.

Thinking of knowledge and ignorance in terms of building a shelter or a prison is helpful in understanding the virtue of truth. The famous passage of scripture says "the truth shall make you free." [1] It is also often said that truth or "knowledge" is access to power. Both of these maxims are in fact describing the same principle. To the extent that a person is ignorant of forces in his environment (like the man walking off the roof), he is "acted upon" by them and brought into some degree of captivity, rather than maintaining his ability to freely and willfully direct his action. To the degree that he has knowledge and understanding of laws and dynamics in operation, he will have the power to negotiate and to overcome these forces and thereby possess greater power to enact his own intentions as opposed to being in a state of ignorance about them.

The difference between a shelter and a prison is that while the shelter keeps a person free from external dangers, the prison cuts him off from beneficial things. Ignorance does one of two harmful things: It causes a person to either fail to include protections where they are necessary, or to place limitations where they are unnecessary. Thus, the shelter of truth and knowledge is access to the power to overcome the forces that limit freedom. Knowledge is access to power and power is access to freedom. Truth, therefore, not only sets one free but also keeps one safe from harm.

CONSTRUCTING REALITY

Building a personal structure of reality is such a uniquely personal process that determinations derived from experience or drawn from other sources become as significant a part of identity as the experience itself. Once determinations are made, they become hard to alter, as doing so requires a reconfiguration of personal identity. Consequently, whether a person is living in a shelter of accurate information or a prison of fiction, it is easy to become attached to any principle of understanding that gives his current life meaning or a sense of security. The structure of personal reality undergoes transformation every time he adds, alters, or lets go of a belief or a description of himself or his world. Sometimes this process happens so gradually that he does not even notice the change. Other times, when he must alter or relinquish a principle of understanding that he has held for a long time, or that is widely accepted by other people, he is more attached to it and may even experience some grief to let it go.

When so much is invested in structures of personal reality, a person can easily be offended when his beliefs are challenged because he feels like he is being told "You built your shelter incorrectly," "Your shelter has no roof " or "You built yourself a prison, not a shelter! People are quite invested in the structures they have built, for they have lived in them for some time, roof or no roof, shelter or prison. Ideological discord exists at every point at which human beings have differences in their structures of reality. The areas of greatest structural difference between people are those that have produced the most conflict at every level of human relationship and interaction – personal, societal, and national.

One of the areas of greatest structural difference among people is belief concerning unseen and intangible realities – those principles that cannot easily be proven to be true or false by research or experimentation. Some of these beliefs include whether a person's consciousness will cease or continue after biological death, whether human existence is purposeful or random, and many other important aspects of knowledge that affect self-conception. These beliefs are far-reaching and affect many other areas of life. They affect a person's beliefs about war, politics and life purpose. They affect every belief that a person holds about himself, other people, other nations, moral judgments, values, priorities, and every other aspect of life. They represent the portion of personal reality most heavily responsible for determining an individual's potential for joy and fulfillment.

Therefore, a person's beliefs regarding unseen realities may have more formative power over his identity and action than his understanding of many concrete and tangible things. As a person's identity is deeply entwined with his understanding of the nature of reality, it makes sense why so much blood has been spilt over religious difference. When any object of personal identification is attacked, it is easy to feel attacked personally. Beliefs about God and life purpose are some of the most precious objects of identity that human beings possess.

Therefore, the investment of identity in any belief allows a perceived attack of that belief to feel equivalent to a personal assault, potentially deserving of retaliation.

Peter Rollins, a writer from Ireland – a location known historically for religious violence between Protestants and Catholics – distinguishes "right belief" from the manner in which a person holds their beliefs. He points out that from a position of doctrinal certainty, the two primary modes of interaction between people of different beliefs are "consumption", trying to mold another's beliefs into one's own, or rejection of the other and/or their beliefs altogether. [2] Both of these modes of operation serve to protect the portion of personal identity that is entwined with belief.

The possibility of an even exchange in which two people can openly share their beliefs without such protection occurs less often. Being open to accepting a new belief or to changing an old one requires allowing personal identity to be vulnerable to transformation. At some point in life, most people choose to protect their identity from any change and the insecurity of the conceptual upheaval and reorientation that accompany this transformation. The building tools which construct personal reality are put away, and the structure of personal reality may have an alarm system put in place to prevent any change to cherished belief.

When a person's beliefs are protected in this manner, they become filters through which new experiences are perceived and understood. When a new experience enters after a filter is already in place, no new evaluation can be made and the information gets placed into existing categories of understanding. This tendency explains why people become set in their longstanding perceptions and patterns of behavior, the way they have always seen and done things. The desire for stability and security work against the inclination to grow, change, and progress. When confronted with new or foreign ideas, people are much more likely to keep rooms exactly the same than they are to get out the construction tools and start a conceptual remodeling project.

Each person's structure of reality has been built and protected along a continuum between the extremes of "rigid protection" and "open remodeling". Some builders of personal identity have kept their tools close by and are ever open to exploring new remodeling ideas, allowing their structure of reality to be continually transformed and altered. Others protect conceptual identity not only with an alarm system but also maintain a team of security guards ready to shoot down any new idea that might threaten their current precepts of understanding before it even has a chance to approach. Such protection is inherently in opposition to the nurturing of truth.

The nature of every correct principle is that it not only withstands scrutiny and investigation, but grows stronger from it. Truth does not have need for any defense or protection. Truth has no weakness, nothing to hide. When any principle is authentically investigated, one of three things can happen:

1) Additional physical, rational, or intuitive evidence is discovered which further confirms or validates the truth of the principle.
2) No new information about the principle is discovered.

Or...
3) New information is discovered that does not support the principle, or in fact refutes it.

In the first case, a person's understanding of truth is deepened, in the second there is no change, and in the third, fallacy that was being taken as truth will be able to be distinguished. The only real enemies to a person's understanding of truth are, therefore, pride, insecurity, and exhaustion. Pride entices a person to believe in the perfection of her positions in protection of the portion of her identity rested upon them. Insecurity motivates her to cling to her longstanding beliefs out of fear of losing the conceptual stability they provide. Exhaustion comes when she simply does not possess the energy to undergo change of conceptual understanding. One or more of these enemies of truth have visited most people either in moments or as constant companions.

For a person to have the incentive to choose "Truth" over its enemies, it must be seen as providing greater comparative benefit. Adherence to familiar belief provides clear benefits, but what can Truth give to the individual? The answer is that understanding natural laws gives access to power to negotiate with the forces and dynamics which bear effect on human life. The power to negotiate with these dynamics is a requisite for human freedom as ignorance of a law in operation leaves one more vulnerable to being acted upon by it. Finally, this freedom from the potential captivity of ignorance, is a requisite for the possibility for human happiness, as the nature of the active human will does not allow it to experience joy when it is enslaved or held captive in any fashion. It experiences joy in direct proportion to the degree to which it stands as a free and willful actor. Overcoming fear and pride in the pursuit of truth offers the only path for any person possessing the ultimate goal of achieving a deep and abiding sense of internal peace and joy.

Principles that are the root of conscious action in the world are the very point of access whereby it can be transformed. As such, discussing principles of knowledge where discord lies is the only way to bring harmony of understanding. Unseen realities are some of the greatest pieces of the puzzle of the whole of all truth; therefore, it is critical to find concrete ground to speak about abstract and intangible truths in order to bring peace and harmony within human action, priority and purpose. The following chapters of the book will discuss concrete evidences that relate to spiritual things. At the end of each section, there will be a short summary of principles discussed and reflective exercises to incorporate them, where desired, into one's conceptual framework or structure of reality.

BUILDING PRINCIPLES:

- All people live in obedience to principles which accurately depict laws and dynamics which bear affect on human life - such as those that concern physical health and safety.
- Knowledge of these laws increases security and power to negotiate with laws in operation in order to direct personal will, rather than to be at their affect.
- Correct principles will withstand scrutiny and investigation.

REMODELING EXERCISES:

- What are the primary sources of information that comprise the material from which you have built your structure of reality?
- Are there any principles which you have accepted into your structure based entirely upon faith in their source?
- Are there particular areas of your structure that you are interested or willing to explore, or others where you are not?

2

The Principle of Identity

THE HUMAN ENERGY FIELD

Perhaps the greatest ideological divide in human structures of reality, has been between those who believe that human consciousness is entirely encapsulated within the brain, and therefore dies at the time of death, and those who believe that some aspect of the human being will survive the death of the physical body. Difference of belief on this point leads to entirely different structures of reality, which in turn dictate an individual's personal values and sense of purpose. Yet there is finally a possibility for this great rift in human understanding to be healed. Scientific evidence of a conscious, sentient energetic body, permeating and surrounding the human physical body, and that may be the aspect of consciousness capable of withstanding the death of the physical body as in the well documented phenomenon of Near Death Experiences (NDEs), provides possible explanation for one of the most important religious or spiritual beliefs of all, the existence of an immortal soul. [1]

It was not long ago that people who believed in unseen electromagnetic fields were considered superstitious. Even when the effects of these fields could be witnessed, many people maintained skepticism in their existence until the fields could be clearly measured. Today the medical profession understands that humans have electromagnetic fields and use this knowledge in medical practice. Doctors use electrocardiographs to make electrocardiograms (EKGs) which are essentially records of the electrical activity of the heart. Electroencephalograms (EEGs) are used to record the electrical activity of the brain. It is easy to forget how many realities of the unseen world recently attacked as delusions, are now universally accepted realities.

The Human Energy Field (HEF) is now in that same place that human electromagnetic fields used to be. It is not something that can be easily measured and is not well known or accepted. But a variety of unconventional methods and instruments have been used to measure and verify its existence. "Dr. Victor Inyushin at Kazakh University in Russia has done extensive research with the human energy field since the 1950s. Using the results of these experiments, he suggests the existence of a 'bioplasmic' energy field composed of ions, free protons, and free electrons. Since this is a state distinct from the four known states of matter- solids, liquids, gases, and plasma— Inyushin suggests that the bioplasmic energy field is a fifth state of matter." [2] In 1979, another scientist, Dr. Robert Becker of Upstate Medical University in New York, "mapped a complex electrical field on the body which is shaped like the body and the central nervous system. He named this field "the direct current control system" and found that it changes shape and strength with physiological and psychological changes. He also found particles moving in this field that are the size of electrons." [3]

Some of the most notable research on the Human Energy Field has been performed by Valerie Hunt, a professor of kinesiology at UCLA: "she discovered that a device used to measure the electrical activity in the muscles called an electromyograph (EMG) can measure the electrical presence of the HEF: Hunt used the electromyograph first to test the frequency of the brain, heart, and other muscles and areas of the body. In addition to these, Hunt discovered that the electromyograph could pick up another field of energy radiating from the body, much subtler and smaller in amplitude than the traditionally recognized body electricities, but with frequencies that averaged between 100 and 1600 cps, and sometimes even higher."[4] These frequencies were much higher than those of the brain, which averaged between 0-30 cps, and the muscles, which averaged 225 cps. The HEF demonstrated the capacity to vibrate at a much faster speed than the physical body. [5]

The Human Energy Field is sometimes referred to as an 'energetic body', referencing its possession of a natural form with standard aspects and capacities. One standard aspect of the energetic body is a circulatory system through which energy flows through meridians, similar to the function the main circulatory system holds for the physical body. [6] A few health and healing modalities such as acupuncture, operate with understanding of this energetic circulatory system; these disciplines maintain that just as healthy blood flow is important to the physical body, flow of energy through the meridians to the entire field is a process of importance to energetic health and function. Energetic organs represent another standard and measurable aspect of the Human Energy Field, energy centers which Eastern schools of thought have long understood to be part of the spiritual anatomy of an individual. When Western experiments have tested these "energetic organs", "instead of emanating from the brain, heart, or muscles, the field was strongest in the areas of the body associated with the chakras."[7]

Natural capacities of the energetic body are often referred to as HSP, or High Sensory Perception, and include capabilities such as intuitive reception of information, energetic sentience, etc. Medical Intuitives have used HSP to diagnose disease through information visible to them within the energetic body of their patients and have their diagnoses verified with traditional instruments. [8] Former NASA Astrophysicist Barbara Ann Brennan, as well as Medical Doctor and PhD Mona Lisa Schulz are medical intuitives and published authors who have each detailed a vast number of specific case examples. In addition, both have had their intuitive and energetically perceptive diagnoses of cancer and other diseases medically verified with a near perfect rate of accuracy. [9]

The movie *Avatar* imagines a world of beings who have evolved beyond the five basic senses, a world where everyone experientially understands their interconnection with all life, and communication can travel in the form of thoughts to be received intuitively. But the capacity for energetic sentience and intuitive function are not fantasy, and these capacities of High Sensory Perception are becoming more common, with tests demonstrating them to be as reliable as the basic human senses of touch, sight or sound. Instruments have been used both to test HSP and to simultaneously measure standard aspects of the Human Energy Field's form, color and composition. Hunt performed an experiment which tested the ability of those who claim to be able to see this subtle energetic body, using an oscilloscope – a device that converts electrical waves into a visual pattern on a monochromatic video display screen:

> "...when an aura reader saw a particular color in a person's energy field, the electromyograph always picked up a specific pattern of frequencies that Hunt learned to associate with that color. She was able to see this pattern on [the] oscilloscope. For example, when an aura reader saw blue in a person's energy field, Hunt could confirm that it was blue by looking at the pattern on the oscilloscope. In one experiment she even tested 8 aura readers simultaneously to see if they would agree with the oscilloscope as well as each other. '[I]t was the same right down the line' says Hunt." [10]

This experiment both uniquely measured certain colors within specific areas of the energetic body, and verified the accuracy of the HSP of the subjects participating in the experiment. Brennan describes her experience as a child in recognizing that she had High Sensory Perception: "I discovered that everything has an energy field around it that looks somewhat like the light from a candle. I also began to notice that everything was connected by these energy fields, that no space existed without an energy field. Everything, including me, was living in a sea of energy...This was not an exciting discovery to me. It was simply my experience, as natural as seeing a squirrel eating an acorn on the branch of the tree." In her lengthy book on the Human Energetic Body, Hands of Light, Brennan explains that this capacity started with seeing colors around people's heads, and with practice she became capable of seeing greater and greater detail within the energetic body.

Skeptics have argued that the research and experimentation that have validated intuitive perception have not been conducted with the rigor that the scientific method requires. In a report requested by the CIA in evaluation of "remote viewing", or the psychic description of a target location being made from a remote site, professor and textbook author Dr. Jessica Utts stated the following:

> "Using the standards applied to any other area of science, it is concluded that psychic functioning has been well established. The statistical results of the studies examined are far beyond what is expected by chance. Arguments that these results could be due to methodological flaws in the experiments are soundly refuted. Effects of similar magnitude to those found in government sponsored research are found [at] a number of laboratories across the world. Such consistency cannot readily be explained by claims of flaws or fraud." [11]

The work Miracles of Mind, written by physicist Russel Targ and Jane Katra, not only provides many concrete evidences of non-local mind but includes a lengthy statement from a member of congress regarding the possibility of fraudulent results:

> "All I can say is that if the results were faked, our security system doesn't work. What these people saw was confirmed by aerial photography. There is no way it could have been faked...Some of the intelligence people I talked to know that remote viewing works, although they still block further work on it since they claim that it is not yet as good as satellite photography..." [12]

Targ and Katra maintain that despite "irrefutable evidence" of intuitive reception of information, such knowledge has been "repressed and ridiculed in Western society because its mechanism is not yet understood." [13] Where capacities of the Human Energy Field had been demonstrated in such cases, without knowledge of the field itself, it makes sense that Western Society has been slower to accept intuitive function. Thankfully, the evidence of the reality of a human energetic body with a standard form and set of capabilities gives a very concrete explanation for capacities that have long been put into the category of 'Para-normal phenomena'. They may be para-normal for a physical body to perform, but are standard and normal capabilities for the energetic body, which every human being possesses.

Yet the most amazing aspect of the Human Energy Field is that it provides an explanation for how consciousness can lie outside the confines of the brain, and how it might be able to withstand the death of the body. Valerie Hunt and others who have measured and seen the Human Energy Field state that it maintains the activity necessary to affect the brain and thereby all other faculties over which the brain has control. When tested, the active power of the Human Energy Field has been demonstrated to respond to stimuli even before the brain does. "[Hunt] has taken EMG readings of the energy field and EEG readings of the brain simultaneously and discovered that when she makes a loud sound or flashes a bright light, the EMG of the energy field registers the stimulus before it ever shows up on the EEG. What does it mean? 'I think we have overrated the brain as the active ingredient in the relationship of a human to the world...It's just a real good computer. But the aspects of the mind that have to do with creativity, imagination, spirituality, and all those things, I don't see them in the brain at all. The mind's not in the brain. It's in that darn field." [14]

BUILDING PRINCIPLES:

- Ideas which seem far-fetched such as the long ridiculed belief in human electromagnetic fields are now widely accepted and used in the practice of medicine.
- Evidence of the human energetic body suggests that human beings do possess a conscious faculty which lies outside the confines of the brain.
- Consideration of principles held within other cultures or schools of thought is a valuable exercise. You may find something to improve your structure of reality that no one in your circle has ever considered or is invested in rejecting.

DISEMBODIED CONSCIOUSNESS

The understanding that human physical bodies are surrounded and permeated with an energetic body may initially seem to be of no great significance or consequence in the debate concerning the existence of an immortal soul. Multiple case studies, however, provide evidence in support of the idea that the Human Energy Field is "self-aware," "conscious," and "sentient;" indeed, evidence has shown that some aspect of the human being is capable of being separated from a live or dead physical body, continuing to have conscious and sentient experiences, and then rejoining with the physical body again. Being independently conscious, there is good evidence that the aspect of consciousness that can withstand death, is the energetic body.

With the progression of life resuscitation technology, there are thousands of documented cases where people have "died," possessing no heart or brain activity, and later returned to relate stories of continued consciousness during these periods of "death". The formal term used to classify such an experience is "Near Death Experience" (NDE) and was first used by Dr. Raymond Moody, in the book *Life After Life* in reference to a subjective experience related by persons who had been resuscitated from, or come very near to, death. [15] The International Association for Near Death Studies maintains an extensive and growing database of NDE cases and a wealth of information for those seeking to investigate the phenomenon. [16] NDEs are reported in about 1/3 of people who have had their life resuscitated, and Raymond Moody reports that he had "talked with several persons who were adjudged clinically dead years apart, and reported experiencing nothing on one of the occasions, but having quite involved experiences on the other."[17]

While the term "near death" seems to describe a state approaching death, many cases move into territory that were it not for the subject's miraculous recovery, the state would very well have been defined in much more permanent terms, such as "clinical" or "brain" death: "[U]nder normal circumstances whenever a person talks, thinks, imagines, or does just about anything else, their EEG registers an enormous amount of activity...even hallucinations measure on the EEG. But there are many cases in which people with flat EEGs have had NDEs. Had their NDEs been simple hallucinations, they would have registered on their EEG." [18] This is important, because there has been very recent research that claims that when people first die, their brain is still functioning, and they know of this fact. They may hear the doctor pronounce them dead, and then later be resuscitated and relate that story. Until this research, those stories of people hearing themselves declared dead, was evidence of the soul, or of consciousness persisting after death. It no longer is. But as stated in the above quote, many NDEs have occurred in which there was no brain activity, demonstrating that this new research cannot explain it all away as being memories of a brain that was still functioning after physical death.

Beyond this, many NDEs contain out of body experiences, where the consciousness travels away from the dead physical body and overhears conversations that are later described as accurate depictions of events their brain was nowhere near, to be able to process. Similarly, some NDEs contain travel to a supernatural realm, with many more aspects of experience that can be analyzed to determine their authenticity as experience of a human brain, or a disembodied aspect of human consciousness.

The initial problem with NDEs was that they were completely subjective experiences and very difficult to verify. Due to the difficulty in verifying the authenticity of the NDE, scientists postulated alternative physiological and psychological explanations for what was occurring. For years these experiences were reduced to being a last-attempt fantasy of the human mind to hang onto life, with the visual imagery some described during the period of near death being attributed to hallucination, and other aspects of the experience being attributed to productions of various parts of the brain. As medical resuscitation techniques have continued to improve, and reports of NDEs have continued to grow, medical doctors began to do further research on the aspects of the NDE that could be verified, and the specific claims NDE patients make regarding things that they have seen or witnessed during the period of "near death".

Trained at Johns Hopkins University, Dr. Melvin Morse first became interested in such phenomena after witnessing the recovery of a seven year old drowning victim who was resuscitated and had an NDE during that period. [19] Morse was skeptical but fascinated and did studies researching NDEs in children. [20] He conducted interviews of hundreds of children who related verifiable conscious experiences that took place during the period that they were declared dead:

"I interviewed children who had left their dead bodies

on emergency room tables and 'floated' to the waiting room to visit with their concerned families. Later, they were able to recall conversations and scenes that they could not possibly have witnessed in their comatose state." [21]

The reason for providing this example, is that a child who left their dead body on the ER table, and floated to another room, heard conversations they were able to verify as accurate when away from the physical body. So it cannot be said that their brain was still functioning, and overheard the conversation.

Scientists call these verifiable aspects of the NDE "veridical perceptions", perceptions of specific and unique events that can be verified as true or false. Veridical perceptions are often accurate depictions of events that the NDE experiencer's (NDEr's) physical body could not have seen or heard and that the NDEr could not have figured out through logic or reasoning skills. The veridical perceptions normally happen in stages of the NDE where the subjects experience themselves in surroundings considered part of the "natural" world. Moody reports a case in which a woman left her body during surgery, traveled to the waiting room, and saw that her daughter was wearing mismatched plaid clothes. While the mother did not see her daughter that day physically, she later mentioned this to her maid, who was astonished to hear how she knew this fact and explained that she had dressed the woman's daughter so hastily that she had not noticed the mistake. [22]

Moody says that there are maybe 15 elements of the Near Death Experience, such as hearing oneself pronounced dead, traveling through a tunnel, finding oneself outside of their physical body and watching the resuscitation attempt being made by doctors. Then the experiencer notices that he still has a body, but one of a very different nature, is visited by the spirits of relatives and friends who have already died, and encounters a spirit demonstrating love beyond description, or a being of light, then is asked a question to "make him evaluate his life", and is shown a review of his life, etc. Sometimes the experiencer comes to a point of no return, which if he passes, he will have to stay in the spirit world, and is told he must return to earth. Finally he reunites with his physical body, and experiences bodily sensations of pain, etc. again. [23] Moody says that nobody he interviewed experienced all 15 elements of the experience, but many have reported 8 or more. Moody also reports that these common elements of the NDE are given by people of various "religious, social and educational backgrounds". [24]

> *"I interviewed children who had left their dead bodies on emergency room tables and 'floated' to the waiting room to visit with their concerned families. Later, they were able to recall conversations and scenes that they could not possibly have witnessed in their comatose state."*

In *Life After Life*, Moody goes through the main elements of the experience, and shares individual stories which coincide with that element. The stories of the Out of Body aspect of the experience, are a testimony of human consciousness not being encapsulated entirely within the brain. One individual states:

> "When I looked I saw blinding lights, the headlights of a car that was speeding towards us. I heard this awful sound-- the side of the car being crushed in-- and there was just an instant during which I seemed to be going through a darkness, an enclosed space. It was very quick. Then, I was sort of floating about five feet above the street, about five yards away from the car, I'd say and I heard the echo of the crash dying away. I saw people running up and crowding around the car, and I saw my friend get out of the car, obviously in shock. I could see my own body in the wreckage among all those people, and could see them trying to get it out. My legs were all twisted and there was blood all over the place." [25]

Another woman relates:

> "I stopped, floating right below the ceiling, looking down. I felt almost as though I were a piece of paper that someone has blown up to the ceiling. I watched them reviving me from up there! My body was lying in plain view, and they were all standing around it. I heard one nurse say, 'Oh my God! She's gone!', while another one leaned down to give me mouth-to-mouth resuscitation." [26]

And it is during the Out of Body Period that many

NDErs relate travel to a supernatural realm, sometimes seeing relatives who have already passed, sometimes meeting a being of light, and going through a life review. Yet even within the supernatural realm, events can happen which can shed light on the authenticity of these experiences. One of these cases involved two individuals who died simultaneously- "as a female NDEr found herself moving through the tunnel, and approaching the realm of light, she saw a friend of hers coming back! As they passed, the friend telepathically communicated to her that he had died, but was being 'sent back'. The woman, too, was eventually 'sent back' and after she recovered, she discovered that her friend had suffered a cardiac arrest at approximately the same time of her own experience. [27]

Some capacities of the Human Energy Field, or whatever aspect of the human being maintains consciousness while disembodied, are gleaned by reviews of NDEs. Many report that during the period where they were separated from their physical bodies they had unusual abilities. Some of these include being able to see through walls, see energetic matter around physical bodies, and "hear" the unspoken thoughts of the people nearby. These unique capabilities of energetic or intuitive discernment are similar in description to living persons who possess heightened energetic or intuitive perceptions referred to as High Sensory Perception, such as those with ability to diagnose diseases through the perception of precursors of disease present in the energetic body, before they are even yet detectable by many traditional diagnostic tests. [28] Living persons who receive accurate information either intuitively or through some capacity of energetic discernment demonstrate a natural capability that is not developed in all living persons, but that is a common experience of those who have experienced a NDE. People who had no special capabilities of energetic perception or intuition in life have these skills in great proficiency in death.

This research gives support to the belief that just as a physical body has natural capabilities such as vision and mobility, so too does the energetic body have capacities unique to being a body of energy. These capacities, associated with a faster vibration of the HEF, are present in living persons who have innately strong or highly developed energetic function. They are similarly present in living souls who have shed the denser matter of the physical body. The physical body therefore seems to present a handicap to some of the natural capacities of the energetic body.

It is often said that considering all possible explanations, science will generally prove the most logical and simple one. The question to answer is how anyone who is physically dead, during the exact period of their physical death, can simultaneously be experiencing events or witnessing things in completely different locations which are later verified to be accurate depictions of events. Saying that some part of the brain is responsible is not a simple or logical answer in the cases where there was no brain activity at the time, or where the brain wasn't around to witness the events. The discovery of the independently conscious human energetic body gives a scientifically measurable and plausible explanation of these phenomena.

NDE travel to realms considered to be "supernatural" has

potential to be seen in terms which accord with principles of energetic frequency and density of matter. [29] Some maintain that reality is multidimensional, and that since the energetic body that remains conscious after death is a much finer substance vibrating at a much higher frequency than the physical body, this body can travel to realms of reality that lower vibrations or denser matter simply cannot. [30] In the same way that fine particles sift through a strainer but large ones are unable to pass through, the energetic body, vibrating at a faster speed than the physical body, has demonstrated the ability to travel to other realms of existence after physical death. After analyzing thousands of NDE experiencers, NDE researcher Kenneth Ring believes that the NDE is travel of the human consciousness to a more pure, higher vibrating dimension, that NDEs are ventures into the more "frequency-like" realms of existence. After an exhaustive analysis of NDEs and alternative explanations, author of The Holographic Universe, Michael Talbot concludes:

> "In brief, when all these facts are considered together - the widespread nature of the NDE, the absence of demographic characteristics, the universality of the core experience, the ability of NDErs to see and know things they have no normal sensory means of seeing and knowing, the occurrence of NDEs in patients who have flat EEGs - the conclusion seems inescapable: People who have NDEs are not suffering from hallucinations or delusional fantasies, but are actually making visits to an entirely different level of reality."[31]

Scientists have not determined conclusively that the human energy field is the conscious body that travels and has experiences during the NDE; but what is undeniable, is that some aspect of a human being disconnects from the physical body at death and continues to see, think and experience. Scientific understanding can now support a principle of human identity that is foundational to almost all religious and spiritual ideologies: Humans are not finite, material beings, but immortal souls who have come into tabernacles of corruptible matter for a sojourn on this earth.

BUILDING PRINCIPLES:

- The human being possesses a soul which will withstand the death of the physical body. The existence of the Human Energy Field provides an explanation for how the human being can persist beyond the death of the brain.
- Near Death Experiences have long been unexplainable, and therefore a great deal of reductionist argument has attempted to place their cause in hallucination, or an activity taking place within the brain as it approaches death.
- Medical doctors and scientific fields of study are beginning to accept the NDE as evidence of post-mortal experience.

ENERGY AND HEALTH

Knowledge of the Human Energy Field has many immediate and far reaching implications. One of the most significant is evidence of the role it plays in physical and emotional health. Research on the correlation between composition of the energetic body and the state of physical and psychological health one possesses has revealed the energetic body to be connected to every aspect of human health. Understanding the factors which affect energetic health is therefore a critical area of human knowledge to be developed in constructing the most secure structure of personal reality.

Systems of detecting radiation from living tissues have now helped to diagnose breast cancer ten years earlier than was previously possible. [32] Some of the initial research in this area was performed by Dr. George De La Warr & Dr. Ruth Brown who developed a system called radionics which enabled them to discern energetic precursors to specific diseases. [33] In support of this evidence, those who are capable of seeing the Human Energy Field explain that while the energetic body differs from person to person, depending on an individual's physical, mental, and emotional states, there are also consistencies within the fields between individuals suffering from a particular disease. Author Michael Talbot summarizes Barbara Ann Brennan's description of this:

> "In the early stages cancer looks gray-blue in the aura, and as it progresses, it turns black. Eventually white spots appear in the black, and if the white spots sparkle and begin to look as if they are erupting from a volcano, it means the cancer has metastasized. Drugs such as alcohol and marijuana and cocaine are also detrimental to the brilliant, healthy colors of the aura and create what Brennan calls 'etheric mucus.'

Prescription drugs are not exempt, and often cause dark areas to form in the energy field over the liver. Potent drugs such as chemotherapy clog the entire field…According to Brennan, a person's emotional and psychological disposition is also a reflection of their energy field. She explains that the colors associated with the frequencies verified on the oscilloscope as well as their intensity, clarity or muddiness and location in the field are related to a person's mental and emotional states, physical activity, and many other aspects of health."[34]

The relationship is so strong that Brennan contends that the most common causes of disease are "psychological and spiritual problems", and that she can see "the effects of a person's negative thoughts, wrong beliefs, and difficult relationships in his or her auric field. Toxic emotions and thoughts, as well as childhood traumas and injuries, manifest as blocks in the flow of energy in a person's aura, or distortions in the rotating colors of the chakras as they pull vital energy into a person." [35] The degree to which the natural aspects of the field such as clarity, brightness, and form are uniformly affected by influences in the environment supports understanding the energetic body as having a natural constitution and being bound by laws which govern its function and well-being.

Anything that has a "nature" or standard attributes can have this nature maintained or distorted by forces that act upon it. The nature of the human lung is its placement within the body, its function of inhalation and exhalation of air, and its composition of pink tissue, ducts that take in air, et cetera.

This nature can be enhanced with aerobic exercise, where the natural capacities of the lung can be increased. Likewise, its nature can be corrupted if smoke and other toxins are taken into its tissues. The natural pink or pure state of the lung can become a black tissue with its function for taking in breath disabled, according to the principles of its natural operation. The terms "purify" and "corrupt" refer to the restoration and distortion of the "nature" of anything that has a natural state. Just as the natural state of a pink lung can be corrupted in terms of its form and function, so too can the natural character and composition of the energetic body be maintained, corrupted, or purified.

The effect of the energetic environment upon matter and other fields of energy for health or detriment, has also been supported through now famous experiments conducted by Dr. Masuro Emoto on the formation of water crystals. Dr. Emoto simultaneously exposed water to loving and harsh expressions, complete indifference, classical music, violent media, and other types of energetic frequencies with startling results. He found that the process of the formation of the water crystal was greatly affected by the energetic content of its environment. Those formed in the presence of love and uplifting vibrations formed beautiful structured crystals resembling intricately patterned snowflakes. Those formed in the presence of negativity formed deformed crystals or no crystals at all. [36] Considering that the human body is largely composed of water, the effect of these frequencies on singular molecules is representative of what human beings expose themselves to in the presence of different types of energy fields in daily life. One's personal energy field is constantly in a state of exchange with the external environment. This is why someone can feel a sense of invigoration being in a beautiful spot in nature where there is more life emanating energetic vitality, or feel a depletion of energy going into an old office with an entirely different quality of energetic content.

This research supports and aligns with religious and spiritual theology that teach purification of thought and action, and encourage surrounding oneself with uplifting and positive influences. In the same way that caring for one's physical body requires the conscious attempt to take in nutritious food rather than toxins, caring for one's energetic body requires the conscious attempt to place oneself in healthy energy fields and to avoid toxic energetic environments. This does not mean that someone should never spend time with their angry, fearful, or anxious friend or family member, or can never again have a negative thought. It simply means to be conscious about the fields one places their energetic body into, in the same way that it is wise to be conscious about the foods that one takes into their physical body. Many times people will say "I would never put such a thing into my body", but would not even think twice about allowing something much worse near their energetic body.

Someone with generally healthy eating habits who on one day eats a deep fried, high cholesterol food is not going to notice any undesirable effect or have a have a heart attack as a result. But if like in the movie *Supersize Me*, a healthy person suddenly ate nothing but fast food for a month, he would notice negative effects to his short and long term physical health. Similarly, if someone generally places his energetic body in healthy environments but here and there spends time with an energetically negative person, or listens to an aggressive song, he may or may not see a noticeable effect. But if he spends a good degree of time in an unhealthy energetic environment, such as a toxic environment at work or at home, or develops a pattern of exposing himself to media with negative or impure content, the health of his energy field will be affected.

Alternatively, surrounding oneself with positive energetic influences has been demonstrated to have very clear, measurable affects on the composition of the energetic body. Those who have had NDEs and reported being in a more pure, higher frequency level of existence, have had very dramatic effects to their energetic health and function upon return. Many report new energetic sensitivities which correlate to specific capacities of High Sensory Perception. In his study of people who have had such experiences, Morse noted that NDE groups reportedly had more than four times the number of validated psychic experiences as did the well or seriously ill groups of people with whom they were compared. He described many instances wherein people who had experienced light as part of their NDE were surprised by influxes of pre-cognitive information, clairvoyant vision, and healing ability after their experiences. [37]

Additionally, upon return most have difficulty with loud or discordant sounds, supporting Emoto's findings regarding the energetic quality and effect of the vibration of words and music. Most NDEers prefer classical or melodic music, and recognize the effect of the type of music one listens to upon the level of health and peace experienced by the energetic body. [38] It was also documented that some NDEers noticed that the composition of their energetic field now affects nearby electrical equipment. "Usually sporadic in effect and impact, some experiencers have noticed: watches can stop, microphones 'squeal,' tape recorders quit, television channels change with no one at controls, light bulbs pop, telephones 'drop off,' computers suddenly lose memory..."[39] On occasion, NDEers experience surges of energy up and down the spinal column through which the 'energetic organs', or charkas, are aligned, giving further evidence of the reality of these energetic organs and their role in spiritual function. [40] NPR's award winning religious correspondent Barbara Bradley Hagerty cites research demonstrating the energetic body's travel to another dimension can 'transform a person physically'. She gives example of structural changes found in the brain of NDEers after returning which correlate to these new spiritual sensitivities and capacities. This demonstrates the miraculous principle that the health of the energetic body truly is primary to that of the physical body. [41]

BUILDING PRINCIPLES:

- The energetic body has been measured to have a direct correlation to physical and emotional health.
- The energetic environment has been measured to have a formative effect upon the energetic body. Energetic bodies which have traveled to higher planes of existence have demonstrated increased function in areas traditionally known as 'High Sensory Perception'.

3

The Principle of the Whole

THE WHOLE

When one looks out at a crowd and sees hundreds of separate physical frames, the understanding that a field of energy surrounds each individual, permeating the fields of others, allows this crowd of individuated people to be seen, at another level of reality, as an interconnected whole. Children are taught in early science courses that while matter in the physical world looks to be composed of objects that possess measurable dimensions and locations in space, what is seen with the eye is not always the most accurate picture of reality. If matter is broken into smaller and smaller pieces, the point is eventually reached where those pieces – electrons, protons, etc. – no longer possess the traits of dimension or locality. They simply no longer have any definite measurable shape or specific location in space.

Over the last few decades, scientists and authors have noted that the "wave-particle duality" is evidence of this seemingly illogical, paradoxical phenomenon: If an electron is shot at a piece of glass, it may hit the glass at one single point and break through as one solid particle, but it can just as easily dissolve into a wavelike cloud of energy and hit many different points simultaneously. Physicists have determined that electrons simply do not possess the measurable dimension or location of objects. [1] While at the level of our everyday reality, in our coarse sensory perception, things seem to have specific locations, at a more subtle level of reality, location ceases to exist. Physicists call this property non-locality, which evidences interconnectedness to all matter and life. [2] Even if there are distinct subatomic particles, they are connected to each other, overlapping at various points in space. At times, in fact, groups of individual electrons behave like interconnected wholes. Of this phenomena, physicist Dr. David Bohm states, "electrons are not scattered...the whole system is undergoing co-coordinated movement more like a ballet dance than like a crowd of unorganized people." He notes that "such quantum wholeness of activity is closer to the organized unity of functioning parts of a living being than it is to the kind of unity that is obtained by putting together the parts of a machine."[3]

The science of interconnectedness demonstrates that each individual part affects the whole in which it is contained. Within the human body, a subtle imbalance in one area can affect other systems and the health of the whole body. When an undesirable symptom arises in any one area of a whole, its cause may be due to connection and interaction with other parts of the same. The weakness of seeing a whole as being many disconnected parts is that problems that arise from the connection and interaction of those parts will not have their true causes addressed. This leaves those who would desire a permanent solution unable to find one and left only to try to mitigate the undesirable effects of the symptoms. For this reason, Bohm argues that:

> "Our almost universal tendency to fragment the world and ignore the dynamic interconnectedness of all things is responsible for many of our problems, not only in science but in our lives and our society as well. For instance, we believe we can extract the valuable parts of the earth without affecting the whole. We believe it is possible to treat parts of our body and not be concerned with the whole. We believe we can deal with various problems in our society, such as crime, poverty, and drug addiction, without addressing the problems in our society as a whole."[4]

THE HUMAN WHOLE

In the same manner that the greater universe is composed of various interacting parts, the human being is multi-dimensional, possessing various aspects which interact and affect each other. In recent years, there has been an increasing awareness of how the mind affects physiology, and increased acknowledgement of the role of psychological stress in the production and exacerbation of disease. The understanding that human beings possess a body of energy that affects the mind, body, and emotions must necessarily affect the practice or medicine and psychiatry. And on this note, some positive and inspiring changes are beginning to occur, such as in the increasingly common practice of including art and music therapy in psychiatric wards. As these professions exist to promote and ensure the physical, mental, and emotional well being of their patients, greater inclusion and application of these principles of health into medical and psychiatric practice will represent a huge step forward in pursuing these outcomes.

Where this knowledge is currently absent, such as in cases of child behavioral problems and adult mood disorder where brain chemistry is seen as the single precipitating cause, simply providing a medication to adjust brain chemistry is seen as the best and most logical solution. But if the behavior or emotional disposition is considered within the context of other aspects of the self, such as the physical body and the nutrition it receives, or the energetic body and the quality of its environment, true causes may reveal themselves and allow the problem to be permanently addressed rather than symptoms temporarily treated.

Managing chemistry with drugs is an ongoing process, and in the worst cases, the negative symptoms can remain unchanged or even worsen, such as in cases of adolescent suicide as a result of taking anti-depressants. Humans are multi-dimensional beings possessing physical, emotional, intellectual and spiritual aspects. The physical body is conscious of pain and pleasure, and maintains awareness of many other varieties of sensation. The intellect is mentally conscious of the quality of the emotions, as well as its perceptions about life and "images" of itself, from which stem all of the expectations it places on itself and others. The energetic body is in a constant state of exchange with the fields of energy in its environment. All of these aspects of the self are interconnected and affect each other. When energy and its effects on physiology are considered as potential causes in medical and psychological cases, additional insight into the root cause of the symptoms has often become apparent.

Medical intuitives say that many psychological issues are often caused by "tears, blockages and imbalances in the aura." [5] When people experience an emotional trauma there is often anger, sadness, or even grief that is not processed at the time. The trauma represents an injury in the energy body just like a cut in a physical body. Where an energetic injury is not fully healed there will likely be clear, subsequent, physical or psychological effects. Those who practice energy medicine also recognize that similarly, repressions of daily stress, anxiety, sadness, or anger, can compound over time and turn into large blockages and imbalances in the energetic body which can cause physical or psychological disease or dysfunction.

Understanding the reality of energy and its effect on human health and happiness is a critical beam to include in the structure of personal reality. Many people live in toxic energetic environments where the health and well-being of their energetic body is slowly being diminished and they have no understanding for why they feel energetically depleted, or emotionally anxious or unhappy. Just like the water crystals in Dr. Emoto's experiments that formed beautiful patterns or deformed blobs, human beings have sensitive energetic bodies that thrive and decline based on their energetic environments. Whether one chooses to use the terms "positive and negative" or terms with moral connotation, there is an undeniable and now scientifically measurable difference between love and hate, gentleness and violence, selfishness and generosity, and their effects on the natural composition of the energetic body.

Before such research existed, it was frequently believed that all moral injunctions to love and forgive, to overcome anger and purify one's thoughts, were good principles to live by, but certainly not as important as laws regarding physical safety. But the evidence of these realities and their effects on human health and happiness can no longer be denied. The thoughts we carry day in and day out, the influences of loving or violent fields of energy we allow into our home and cars through music and television programs, are formative and will literally be reflected in the energetic content of our thought patterns, our actions, and eventually the composition of the energetic body.

Years ago, anti-smoking advertisements showed pictures of pink and black lungs to demonstrate the toxic and harmful effects of smoking. Perhaps in the future, sensitive equipment will be able to show an image of an energy field with dim, muddy colors and an imbalanced shape. The commercial will then show people yelling at each other, watching violent movies, maintaining no connection with nature, no time for meditation or prayer. Then another image will be shown, this time of a vibrant and healthy energetic body. The commercial will then show people being loving to each other, taking walks in the park with their pet, listening to uplifting music, praying, etc. Finally words will be spoken: "Let's clean up this world, and help to prevent energy cancer."

> *The understanding that human beings possess a body of energy that affects the mind, body and emotions must necessarily affect the practice of medicine and psychiatry.*

BUILDING PRINCIPLES:

THE PRINCIPLE OF THE WHOLE

- The greater universe is a whole which is composed of smaller interconnecting parts.
- The human being might be said to be a microcosm of this greater whole or a universe within itself, being composed of aspects which interact and affect each other.
- Including knowledge of the human energetic body as one of the primary aspects of the human being represents an evolution in knowledge of the human organism and power to understand the source of its health, drive, and purpose.

CAUSES AND SYMPTOMS

Without knowledge of all aspects of the whole, holistic avenues of healing are unavailable, and the only options that remain in such situations where some causes are unknown, is to treat symptoms of disease directly. The word "symptom" is commonly used to define a manifestation or sign of a particular disease within a system. By this definition, the symptom cannot be "cured" directly as it has a cause outside of itself; the only way to deal with a symptom directly is through treatment, which seeks to mitigate and manage its effects. Symptoms are often treated through attempts at their suppression. This is why so many types of medication have "anti" in their title: anti-inflammatory, anti-biotic, anti- seizure, anti-depressant, anti or "de" contestant, and others. The system is pushing out, and a suppression technique pushes back in. As treatment does nothing to heal the root cause or bring into balance the dynamics within the system that originally produced this symptom, its treatment will frequently result in a new or similar expression of the disease.

As Cell Biologist Bruce Lipton explains: "Every time a drug is introduced into the body to correct function A, it inevitably throws off function B, C, or D." [6]

This is why people commonly go to the doctor to treat the manifest physical symptoms they are suffering from and then find in a few days, weeks, or months that a different type of symptom has arisen. Where the interaction between various aspects of the self produces an undesirable symptom in any area, such as emotional unrest, psychological insecurity, or physical fatigue, all aspects of the self must be examined in order to find the cause or network of causes accountable for the illness or pain. To develop long term health, more than quick fixes must be available and sought after. Modes of healing and transformation must use a holistic approach that will address any singular problem in the context of the whole interconnected organism.

Understanding the root cause or causes behind any event generally requires investigation of multiple factors beyond the obvious. If parents receive a call from their child's principal letting them know that their son or daughter has misbehaved, focus is usually placed on the action or immediate reason that the child ended up in trouble. But there are circumstantial aspects of this child's life that affect their actions. It may seem bizarre to say that the child misbehaving was not the actual cause for his being sent to the principal. But the reasoning here is that if there are other life factors that affect the child's mood, such as her family dynamic and relationships, dietary habits, influence of television programs, music or video games, then more primary causes may be able to be distinguished, revealing the misbehavior to be a mere symptom, not the cause to be addressed.

Chasing after a symptom is difficult because it is necessarily reactive; a symptom occurs and then one deals with it. Television parenting shows, such as "Super Nanny," have demonstrated this principle: When parents are frequently annoyed and frustrated by their child's behavior, they tend to be more reactive than proactive. After the child misbehaves they administer some sort of punishment. They may yell in response to something the child has done. In this television show, professional nanny Joe Frost comes into the home, discerns underlying family dynamics such as parents who are aloof or disconnected from each other, and, by addressing the imbalanced or unhealthy underlying family dynamics, significantly decreases the child's misbehavior. The parents move from reactivity to empowerment by shifting their focus from eliminating undesirable "symptoms" to proactively addressing the dynamics that cause these symptoms. Ignorance of the dynamics of relationships and parts within a whole allows effects to be confused with causes. The most recent event in the causal chain is pinpointed and then attacked as the singular cause of an undesirable symptom, when this "cause" is in fact affected by something outside of itself.

In this manner do human beings chase solutions to problems that have multiple causes by addressing only one of an interconnected network of causes, or by erroneously believing additional effects to be the singular cause. Science once understood cause as the single preceding determinant of an event. What they have more recently acknowledged is that there is frequently a network of interrelated causes that affect each other, often in a very non-linear fashion. As the current medical establishment's pursuit of singular causes is a reflection of operating from an outdated physics worldview, Lipton argues that "the conventional medical establishment has not yet incorporated quantum physics into research or medical school training", and the principles of the interconnected universe which stem from it, "with tragic results." [7] To fight symptoms is to stand in powerlessness; to use symptoms as clues to the underlying causes and imbalances behind them is power to heal, power to affect the whole.

BUILDING PRINCIPLES:

- Symptoms of physical and emotional disease often represent disharmony within the human organism as a whole.
- Direct treatment of symptoms may be critical where symptoms are acute, but ultimately they should be used as clues to uncover underlying dynamics within the life of the individual, or areas where aspects of the human being are not in balance.
- Looking at the big picture, every aspect of one's life that bears impact upon physical, mental and emotional health, is a more effective approach to health than focusing singularly on immediate symptoms.

4

The Principle of Character

NATURE, NURTURE, AND ENERGY

Beyond its influence in human health, tests of the human energetic body are helping to resolve the long-standing debate regarding whether genetic makeup, environmental influence, or willfully intended action have most formative power over the character of the individual.

When researchers have examined the degree of freedom or compulsion that a person has, they have come to different determinations. In recent years, many people have argued the case for genetic determinism [1], the belief that genetic dispositions have so much influence on human thought and choice that they may comprise the most primary aspect of human character. But, as mentioned in chapter 2, when tested, the Human Energy Field has been shown to respond to external stimuli even before the brain does. [2] The research of Barbara Hagerty of NPR supports this discovery; her research discusses spiritual practices which can affect structural aspects of the brain. [3]

While many doctors and scientists have long advocated, "biology's Central Dogma- the belief that life is controlled by genes"[4], Cell Biologist Bruce Lipton claims that his research offers "incontrovertible proof that biology's most cherished tenets regarding genetic determinism are fundamentally flawed."[5] In support of new understanding that energetic influences in the environment are of greatest impact to human life, affecting the mind, body and emotions, Lipton states that:

> "...a cell's life is controlled by the physical and energetic environment and not by its genes. Genes are simply molecular blueprints used in the construction of cells, tissues, and organs. The environment serves as a "contractor" who reads and engages those genetic blueprints and is ultimately responsible for the character of a cell's life. It is a single cell's 'awareness' of the environment, not its genes, that sets into motion the mechanisms of life." [6]

He explains that "epigenetics, the study of the molecular mechanism by which environment controls gene activity"[7], a scientific discipline pursuing more advanced understanding of the network of causes beyond mere chemical makeup that affect human life, is "one of the most active areas of scientific research." [8] In this debate regarding whether the human being is essentially free or determined: "On one side of the line is a world defined by Neo-darwinism, which casts life as an unending war among battling, biochemical robots. On the other side of the line is the 'New Biology' which casts life as a cooperative journey..."[9]

In complete contrast to the belief that our cellular structure is a genetic product with no ability to transform beyond its makeup, epigentics has shown that a human being is composed of "smart cells" that are "imbued with intent and purpose; they actively seek environments that support their survival while simultaneously avoiding toxic or hostile ones." While the energetic environment is fundamentally important and affects physiology, this research demonstrates that at a cellular level, human beings seek environments that will be energetically nurturing to them, attempting to shape their energetic composition rather than to merely be shaped by genetic disposition. [10] This research and research of the HEF responding prior to the brain demonstrate that the same aspect of the human being that possesses all properties necessary to be an immortal soul, the Human Energy Field, is not only a free and active agent, but is also the most important of all dimensions of consciousness. It possesses the power to rule both itself and the physical body in which it lives.

BUILDING PRINCIPLES:

- Our cells posses an innate drive to search to find environments that support their health and survival.
- The Human Energy Field responds to its environment prior to the brain, supporting the spiritual premise that human beings possess an aspect

of consciousness which is not under the direction of any other.
- The human energy field can rule itself, possessing the freedom and ability to direct action beyond influences of biology and genetics.

ENERGETIC CHARACTER

The understanding that humans have a body of energy that dwells within the physical body is a principle through which many other aspects of human experience can be explained. The physical body is driven by physiological impulses and attuned to states of physical pleasure or pain. The energetic body is driven by desire for wholeness and attuned to states of peacefulness and anxiety, joy and misery. When an energetic body comes into a physical one, it comes into an instrument which possesses strong innate drives and inclinations which seek fulfillment. In order to secure the continual fulfillment of its needs, the physical body must enlist the support of the active human aspect—the energetic body, or soul. The term "soul" will frequently be used going forward to refer to the collective entity of the energetic body, energetic organs, and any other aspect of the human spiritual body that may as of yet be unknown to us.

The relationship of these two bodies to each other can be one in which the energetic body possesses power to direct its physical instrument according to its will. It can also be a relationship in which the soul subjects itself to the direction of the physical body, in fact becoming a passive or captive agent if it is driven by biological impulse or inclination. For this reason, a biblical passage gives the direction: "In your patience possess ye your souls"[11], teaching each to seek to willfully control or direct their own soul and not submit it to the possession and direction of forces which act upon it.

In scientific support of this principle, Dr. Emoto explains that while "Most of the objects found in nature emit stable frequencies," [12] human beings are unique in their capacity for energetic variance, the degree to which they both affect and are affected by the energetic content of their environment. [13] He describes being less energetically static or stable as a "double edged sword" since human beings can more easily affect each other and the environment for either positive or negative influence. Being more acutely affected by the energetic content of the environment makes a person's primary relationships one of the most important factors in the health of their energy field.

Of all the discoveries regarding the Human Energy Field that relate to its character or composition, perhaps the most astonishing is that it can be positively or negatively affected by human thought. "Dr. William A. Tiller and his colleagues at Stanford University developed a subtle energy detector – an ultra-sensitive Geiger counter-type device – and were able to determine that this subtle energy field responds to intentional human focus."[16] In 1959, Dr. Leonard Ravitz at William and Mary University showed that the Human Energy Field fluctuates with a person's mental and psychological stability. He suggested there is a field associated with thought processes. He suggested that variation of this thought field caused psychosomatic symptoms." [17]

Brennan's assertion that she can see the effect of a person's 'negative or toxic thoughts' as well as wrong beliefs, in distortions within the HEF demonstrates that effect upon one's energetic character is slowly built through the thoughts one maintains over the course of daily life. As the energetic body's most constant companion, if the messages sent by a person's thoughts are a loving wave, they will serve to elevate and purify the field. If they are of self-degradation and negativity towards life and other people, the energy field's natural and vibrant color will dim and its level of vibration will be affected. When people talk about "the power of positive thinking" they rarely realize how literally this is true. The scriptural premise that "as a man thinketh in his heart, so is he" [18] is literally true as thought comes to affect the actual composition of the soul.

BUILDING PRINCIPLES:

- The energetic body responds to intentional thought. Direction of thought, therefore, represents a way for the individual to control and affect the state of their energetic body.

FREEDOM AND HAPPINESS

The possibility for persistent happiness is a direct function of the freedom of the soul. If the energetic body is captive to the forces that act upon it, its freedom to pursue its intentions can be diminished or even destroyed. Any kind of addiction is a testament to this principle, that the free and deliberate activity of the human will can be brought into captivity by biology or emotion. Those who can see the Human Energy Field, and have proven this ability through the correspondence of their descriptions with instruments measuring its frequency and color, have stated that any time that an individual has an addiction to a substance or is ruled by an emotional pattern of behavior, these things are evident in their fields of energy. [19]

The primary energetic influences operating upon the energetic body gain increased power over it as they slowly alter its composition. If an individual listens persistently to aggressive music, her energetic body is being continually influenced by the vibration of aggression. Over time, her field is altered and becomes a reflection of its most prominent energetic influence. In casual expression when people say that a particular song resonates with an experience, memory, or state of emotion, they are describing the way they are affected by its frequency or quality of vibration. The soul can seek out energetic experiences and stimulation which resonate with its current character, often working to maintain or magnify its current energetic composition; alternatively it can pursue relationships, experiences, and stimulation which encourage it to evolve into the character one intends. Choices about the friendships and influences one maintains are often made based on the conscious or unconscious recognition of the effect that they have upon one's life and character.

In the course of everyday life, each of us is exposed to external energy fields of various content and quality which come from many sources outside of ourselves, such as parents and primary relationships, television content, popular music, etc. The energetic fields in the environment are a combination of positive and negative, or those that nurture and those that destroy. To some degree, each person can, with care and intent, attempt to make his energetic environment as nurturing as possible by limiting exposure to negative energetic fields such as fear, lust, greed, and anger. At the same time, it is impossible to shelter ourselves completely from energetic toxins, since each of us is connected to the energetic whole of the human race, where at any given time all manner of wars are being fought, all manner of violence, fear, lust, greed, intolerance, and anger are present.

As a person's energetic body is in a state of constant interaction and exchange with her energetic environment, the quality of her own field either affects another or is affected itself in each and every one of these interactions. Most individual energetic bodies, without active intention to maintain the purity and health of their field, become a reflection of the predominant energtic bodies surrounding them. Unless the soul actively seeks out influences of purity and creates a nurturing environment, its character will not be of its own making, and the person may very likely become someone she would not have chosen to be.

In this manner, forces that act upon a person can slowly gain increased power within his energetic body, having literally become a part of it. Every act of submission to such forces gives them greater power over his very soul and further transforms him into something wholly other then the pure body of energy that he first came into his body with. Action is not easily separated from human identity, as actions affect energetic character, becoming part

> *Dr. Emoto explains that while "Most of the objects found in nature emit stable frequencies," human beings are unique in their capacity for energetic variance, the degree to which they both affect and are affected by the energetic content of their environment.*

of our immortal bodies. While these changes in the character of the soul are not irreversible, the greater portion of a person's field that any pattern of behavior becomes, the more power it will have to force him to perform the same actions in the future, creating a spiral that is difficult to overcome. Whenever a person overcomes forces that act upon him, he gains power of energetic activity or the power to maintain his disposition of peacefulness, love, generosity, and humility, in the face of all forces that would make these qualities and experiences difficult to maintain. When increased, this power represents the ability to maintain the character of his soul in the midst of forces which would alter its composition.

As the soul needs every opportunity to create a pure energetic environment for itself, the greatest power that it has immediately available is personal thought. Every single thought that a person maintains has an energetic value that affects the quality and content of the soul. Every generous, humble, loving, pure, kindhearted thought purifies the soul. Every hardhearted, mean-spirited, self-disparaging, fearful, negative, or lustful thought corrupts its quality and dims its vibration. As a person's personal internal monologue is the most constant companion of the energetic body, it is one of the greatest influences on its character. Though we may dwell in the midst of all manner of influences of impurity and hatred and fear, within ourselves we have power to fight and overcome these influences by actively weeding out every negative thought that comes into our minds and instead planting seeds of positivity about ourselves and others.

The character of the energetic body is a literal quality of purity or corruption, tangible aspects of this sensitive field which are evident to all who have the perceptive faculties to see this subtle body of energy. The quality of this field becomes a reflection of its predominant influences, the sources which feed it. For the soul to be a free and active agent, it must fight and overcome those forces which act upon it. Thought is a sword which can fight for purity within one's own field, thereby affecting the whole and all others for good. Every soul has the power to help heal this whole and each other; every soul has the power to love and to be generous, to be selfless and humble, to be honest and virtuous. Every soul has the power to fell negative thoughts and dwell on all that is good and uplifting. The sword of thought is a powerful weapon, more powerful than any gun or knife or missile or bomb. While those weapons have the power to destroy physical bodies, thought has the power to heal or injure souls.

In essence, the soul has a character which is alterable and will remain with us always. Our lives are processes of becoming, as our actions eventually make impressions on our immortal character, whether contributing to the kind and loving and virtuous composition of our souls, or to an energetic character of negativity, bitterness, and contempt. The freedom and power is given to each human being to direct her soul in its process of becoming – power to shape her life, power to shape her immortal character.

BUILDING PRINCIPLES:

- The soul comes into the body with a pure, vibrant energetic body.
- The character of the soul becomes a reflection of the

energetic environment and influences of positive or negative thought it dwells within.
- Each person has the power to affect their immortal character by the choices they make concerning the energetic influences they immerse themselves in, their actions and the thoughts they maintain on a daily basis.

REMODELING EXERCISES:
- What are some of the primary energetic influences that you can distinguish in your life, such as major relationships, music and media, etc.
- Which energetic influences do you notice yourself feeling nurtured by, or feel peaceful or happy as a result of? Are there any which have a negative effect, and if so can they be minimized or removed?
- How would you describe your thought-life? Practice actively placing a positive or motivational thought in your mind.

5

The Principle of Intelligence

THE ABILITY TO LOVE

As the quality of thought and emotion a person dwells in most frequently has such formative power over an individual and impacts all others with whom one interacts, understanding the factors which affect one's ability to think positively and act lovingly is of great importance to human understanding. As such, it is a subject into which a great deal of research has been poured by a number of different fields of study. Medical doctors, psychiatrists, and many others have written volumes, not only on the benefits of love and positive thinking, but also on factors affecting individual potential for an active relationship with their state of mind and emotion. This is therefore an area of human understanding where there are many existing premises to consider in the light of new findings such as the reality of the human energy field.

Psychologists have determined that the degree to which a

person accepts and loves himself is the same degree to which he is able to extend love to others; to the extent that he is unloving, judgmental and condemnatory of himself, even unconsciously, he will be unloving, judgmental and condemnatory of other people. "It is a psychological truism that our attitudes toward others are conditioned by our fundamental attitudes toward ourselves."[1] As the product that is yielded through being loved or loving another is a sense of personal worth, many scientists and psychologists have put forth research and articles arguing that:

> "All psychological problems, from the slightest neuroses to the deepest psychoses, are symptomatic of the frustration of this fundamental human need for a sense of personal worth...The depth and duration of the symptomatic problems... are only indicative of the depth and duration of the deprivation of self esteem." [2]

The "self-image" of any human being will therefore be the radical determining factor of all his or her behavior. True and realistic self-esteem is the basic element in the health of the human personality. People act and relate to other people in accordance with the way they think and feel about themselves: "Our interpersonal problems begin with intrapersonal conflicts." [3]

People have often been confused about the term "self-love," thinking that even talking about loving oneself is a synonym for narcissism and selfishness. In reality, selfishness is a symptom of an individual who is in a state of starvation in terms of their need for love. In the same way that someone starving for food does not look to find how they can feed other hungry people but first seeks to feed themselves, someone suffering from a starvation of love thinks only of their own needs. "Selfishness is rooted in the very lack of fondness of oneself...Narcissism, like selfishness, is overcompensation for the basic lack of self-love... He loves neither others nor himself." [4]. For this reason, the people who love themselves the least appear to be selfishly putting themselves above others the most. A person has an excess of love to give to others after she first possesses a love and appreciation for her authentic self. Therefore the commandment to "love thy neighbor as thyself " [5] is an injunction to do both, as a person must love himself in order to be able to love any other. On the importance of self love, author John Powell writes, "There is no doubt in my mind that a deep understanding of and serious effort to achieve true love of self is the beginning of all human growth and happiness."[6]

As souls enter into the physical body and human experience, their energetic bodies receive impressions from their energetic environment. Research on the effects of love on unborn children still in the womb has now demonstrated that the energetic value of sound, thoughts, and emotion can impress or injure a fetus and affect the mind and brain chemistry. Experimentation has demonstrated that "Some forms of depression can also originate in utero ... Usually these are produced by a major loss. For what-ever reason – illness or distraction – a mother withdraws her love and support from her unborn child; that loss plunges him into a depression."[7] Pre-natal evaluations provide evidence that experiences in utero can leave "emotional memories," forming neuronal paths through which the journey back into negative emotion and experience, once first opened, can easily be repeated. "You can see this in the after-effects of an apathetic newborn or a distracted sixteen-year-old; for, like other emotional patterns set in utero, depression may plague a child for the rest of his life. This is why treating infant depressions has recently become one of psychiatry's chief priorities." [8]

These discoveries are causing an increasing number of doctors and psychologists to write books for new parents explaining the need to energetically nurture their baby while in the womb and during the birth process. Many children who have birth memories describe the experience of having the umbilical cord being cut as a necessary but energetically painful one. This further emphasizes the experience of human separateness. One mother shares the account of two of her children: "Emma remembered the unpleasant feeling of having her cord cut (after it has stopped pulsating), which she describes as being 'painful in my heart'. Zoe, at age five years of age, described being attached to a 'love-heart thing'." [9]

There is a new level of recognition that after nine months of the baby being literally inside the mother's body, the transition to being a completely separated person from the mother ought to be one made as delicately as possible, especially given the implication of birth memory and the formative effects of these early human experiences. As a result of this understanding, a growing number of people are banking cord blood or requesting physicians allow the umbilical cord to stop pulsating and to fully give all blood and nutrients in the cord to the child prior to cutting it, as this can represent as much as "20-50% of the total blood volume" of the newborn. [10]

This principle of the need for energetic nurturing holds true after birth and throughout infancy, as the language through which the soul perceives and takes in experience is the energetic language of its environment. As a soul was literally in one body with its mother through pregnancy, after birth it continues to desire human connection, craves it with as much intensity and desperation as it would for food to fill a physical hunger. When this need is properly nourished, the soul will develop a core experience of lovability and demonstrate a life of emotional security and independence. When this need is ignored, the soul may feel some degree of impoverishment of spirit that can leave a deep inner emptiness, and may seek to fill this emptiness with every distraction, substance, and activity one can find to quiet it throughout life. Love is very literally the lifeblood of the soul.

This information needs to be reconciled with the prevalent theories which act as if a baby is incapable of being emotionally scarred and they can be put on regimented sleep and feeding schedules ignoring the infant's requests which conflict with them. Where a child's emotionally expressed need to be held or comforted, to be interacted or connected with, or to be loved is ignored in the face of all fervency of expression, some degree of energetic injury can and likely will occur. Doctors feel confident that no trauma is taking place since, on the mornings after such crying sessions, children often smile normally and act as if no trauma has happened. However, this is not always the case:

> "Some parents find the nighttime crying affects their baby's daytime personality – making him clingy and fussy. Many find that any setback (teething, sickness, missing a nap, going on vacation) sends them back to

the previous night-waking problems, and they must let the child cry it out over and over again." [11]

This research is finally being included in mainstream psychiatric understanding of processes of identity formation and emotional development. A fetus, infant, or child is more vulnerable to being energetically wounded than an adult because they come into existence open and vulnerable, without having set up any defenses or protections. Dr. Thomas Verny expresses this sentiment with the following statements:

> "If loving, nurturing mothers bear more self-confident, secure children, it is because the self-aware 'I' of each infant is carved out of warmth and love. Similarly, if unhappy, depressed or ambivalent mothers bear a higher rate of neurotic children, it is because their offsprings' egos were molded in moments of dread and anguish. Not surprisingly, without re-direction such children often grow into suspicious, anxious, and emotionally fragile adults." [12]

Accepting that forces beyond biology and genetics affect psychology and physiology, that human beings do, in fact, possess bodies of energy affected by their energetic environment, is providing revelations of understanding for many symptoms which had previously unknown causes.

BUILDING PRINCIPLES:

- The energetic body needs love to support its health and well-being in the same way that the physical body needs food and water.
- The soul is intensely affected by its earliest energetic influences.

PREMORTAL EXISTENCE

A nearly universal spiritual premise that is now heavily supported by case studies is the precept that the soul existed before being joined to the physical body. In the book of Jeremiah in the Old Testament, a passage states, "Before I formed thee in the belly, I knew thee."[13] Evidence now demonstrates that preborn and newborn children have capacities of rational thought and reflection, a maturity of intelligence which surpasses any capacity of the brain's development or capacity of language at the time. [14] At the same time, the cases mentioned in this section reference the experience of being "in body" as a new and novel experience which induces excitement, fear, and curiosity. Not only do these cases bring additional strength to the case of the immortal nature of human identity, they testify of the existence of the human soul prior to coming to earth, in harmony with the biblical passage above. Over the last decades, thousands of stories of birth memories have been published and analyzed. Subjects include young children and adults who have these memories surface spontaneously, through a recurrent dream or through accessing unconscious memory. In many cases, the subject remembers being joined to a physical body and having the capability to separate and rejoin with it at will:

"Scientist John Lilly writes of his out of body experience at the time of birth. He felt he was squeezed, trapped, and dying. He 'split off... moved out briefly and watched from the outside,' where he saw his mother struggling to give birth. For several hours he waited and watched as his head was stuck in the birth canal. Suddenly, he says, the head broke through, the baby came out, and he moved back into the baby's body. He says he left his body many times after birth, usually to go 'exploring'."[15] "At times I feel like I'm somewhere in the room witnessing what is going on, and at other times I am the child and seeing from that point of view." [16]

In *Babies Remember Birth*, subjects describe the feeling of being an ageless intelligence that does not identify with this infant body it exists within: "I'm not a baby. I'm old. I'm not any age."[17] Another person describes a similar experience of identifying with their mind and not their new body:

"I felt I knew a lot—I really did. I thought I was pretty intelligent. I never thought about being a person, just a mind. I thought I was an intelligent mind. And so when the situation was forced upon me, I didn't like it too much. I saw all these people acting real crazy. That's when I thought I really had a *more* intelligent mind, because I knew what the situation was with me, and they didn't seem to. They seemed to ignore me. They were doing things to me- the outside of me. But they acted like that's all there was. When I tried to tell them things, they just wouldn't listen, like that noise [crying] wasn't really anything. It didn't sound too impressive, but it was all I had. I just really felt like I was more intelligent than they were."[18]

This statement – "I never thought about being a person, just a mind" – fits perfectly with the biblical precept that God "knew" each soul prior to its being enjoined to a physical body. [19] Furthermore, this individual describes the process of being born as novel, emphasizing the oddity of being interacted with as a physical body and not the mind he possesses and the thoughts he puts forth. While having his physical body attended to, this newborn expressed feeling "ignored" as his conscious thoughts were not perceived or responded to by the doctors. Upon separation from the physical body the energetic body has demonstrated ability to communicate entirely through thoughts expressed and received [20]; claims that it possessed this same ability prior to being attached to a physical body support understanding intelligence and communication in the form of thoughts as inherent capabilities of the energetic body.

One of the most common experiences of the conscious and intelligent energetic body in the home of its new infant physical body is the feeling that one's intelligence is not respected by adults. Most assume that the infant brain does not yet have the capacity for a mature level of conscious reflection, believing conscious faculties to be limited to the function of the brain and brain development: "My desire to say something was strong but I couldn't. I couldn't say anything. I didn't know how. But I wanted to. Everybody was laughing and making me feel bad." [21] Another relates, "I felt a fantastic wisdom when I was held there by my feet, but a frustration that all I could do was scream." [22] These infants have the conscious intention of communicating, but do not have the physical capability to do so.

These stories are only a few of the incredible number of documented cases of developed conscious faculties at work in preborns and newborns. In many cases where parents state never having discussed circumstances surrounding the birth with their children, in a spontaneous moment, the child will share details about their birth which accord perfectly with actual events:

> "One boy said he came out by himself when there was a big cut made by doctors. He also described the circular motion 'round, and round, and round' used to apply antiseptic before incision." [23]

> "On a long car trip, a three-year-old Wisconsin boy suddenly asked from the back seat, 'mom, do you remember the day I was born?' Then he informed her that it was dark and he was up real high and couldn't get through 'the door'. 'I was scared, so finally I jumped and got through the door. Then I was ok.' The mother said the child's report was consistent with the fact that he had remained stuck high in the pelvis through some twenty hours of labor. Then things changed suddenly and he was born in a ten-minute second stage." [24]

> "Another spontaneous revelation from the back seat of a car

came from three-and-a half-year-old Jason. On the way home one night, Jason said he remembered being born. He told his mother that he heard her crying and was doing everything he could to get out. It was 'tight', he felt 'wet' and felt something around his neck and throat. In addition, something hurt his head and he remembered his face being 'scratched up'. Jason's mother said she had 'never talked to him about the birth, never,' but the facts were correct. The umbilical cord was wrapped around his neck, he was monitored via an electrode in his scalp, and was pulled out by forceps. The photo taken by the hospital shows scratches on his face." [25]

"A two-and-a-half year old girl amazed her mother with an account of her birth. First she described her feelings, how cold she was, how many people were in the room, and what her mother and father were doing. Then she said, 'Daddy was afraid to hold me, so he just looked at me and touched me. And you were crying, not 'cause you were hurt, but you were happy.' The report was accurate, and the couple said they had never spoken to the child about birth." [26]

On occasion, these stories contain descriptions of events and statements that the baby's parents never knew, but are verified within medical records or the experience of doctors or others present. One such documented case includes the memory a four-year-old girl who remembered a fact that a family friend assisting with a home birth had never shared. When the mother had left the room to take a bath and the baby whimpered, she breastfed the child and felt immediately guilty that she had been the first to breastfeed the child and not her mother. Years later when the same family friend was baby-sitting a group of children including this child, she asked whether she remembered her birth. In addition to correctly describing the roles of everyone present she leaned to this woman and expressed in a confidential tone that she remembered that she had held her and fed her when she had 'cried and mommy wasn't there." [27] In this manner, memories possessed by children and adults regarding their birth experiences are demonstrated to be unique experiences and not merely the relation of accounts they may have heard from their parents later in life.

One might reasonably ask how a mind can consciously hold intentions and reflect on experience without possessing language. Dr. David Chamberlain, Vice President of the Pre- and Perinatal Psychology Association of North America states that in the attempt to answer this question, "A host of new discoveries show that even preborn children are intelligently organized before the brain has had a chance to develop, and that many of a baby's abilities are innate. Examples are learning, memory, dreaming, expression of personality, and ability to communicate. I think these non-physical, less visible processes are best understood as products of the mind, which follow a different timetable than the brain can react apart from it." [28]

> *A nearly universal spiritual premise that is now heavily supported by case studies is the precept that the soul existed before being joined to the physical body*

In a section of his book entitled, "Mind Over Language", Dr. David Chamberlain goes on to direct parents to improve communication with their young children by letting go of "the myth that language is foundational for thought" [29]. Where understanding of objects, abstract concepts and other realities resides in conceptual form, the argument can be made that as the HEF has demonstrated properties of consciousness, it is independently capable of conceptual reflection apart from the human brain's capacity for spoken language at the time. Again, the capacities of the Human Energy Field provide natural explanation of newborn consciousness that would otherwise seem unbelievable. This evidence, in combination with discovery of the human energy field, demonstrates that human beings have an immortal soul that is not only capable of withstanding physical death, but also possesses consciousness and intelligence when first attached to the physical body. These stories provide further evidence that consciousness is not limited to the brain, and that human souls possess intelligence, personality, and sense of purpose before joining with the physical body.

BUILDING PRINCIPLES:

- As humans, we had intelligence, personality, and sense of purpose before coming to inhabit a physical body.

THE BIRTH OF EXPERIENCE:

Principles regarding the Human Energy Field, and the effect on its character and composition when it is acted upon by love, hate and indifference, testify that where food and water may be life to the physical body, love is life to the soul. When the soul receives a constant stream of unconditional love, its form is purified and its natural capacities are enlarged and expanded. If this source of life is absent, the soul suffers a spiritual disease, manifest and verifiable within the actual body of the energy field, which can translate into any one of the negative emotions and psychological disorders, or physiological dysfunctions or diseases. [30] These premises, now supported by research and experimentation, are in perfect accord with one of the foundational spiritual premises of all time – the concept of an initial state of innocence of each soul prior to coming into a world of pleasure and pain, health and disease, joy and misery, a 'dualistic' world where every quality lies on a continuum with its contrasting compliment.

The scriptural story of the fall from innocence into a dualistic world is taken to be literal by some, symbolic by others, and for some believed to have both literal and symbolic significance. One powerful symbol of this story is the state of a newborn child in contrast to most adults in terms of emotional innocence. When a child is born, she does not possess malice, bitterness, resentment, emotional defenses, pride, aggression, hatred, cynicism, or deception. Yet she comes into an environment which can be harsh and emotionally traumatic, and most people will acquire some range of emotional defenses in order to withstand the non-innocent aspects of their environment. The emotional innocence and vulnerability of infants tells something about the environment in which these souls exist prior to entering the body. It is an environment without energetic harshness, intellectual cynicism or mistrust; it is an environment pure enough to maintain the level of emotional vulnerability with which children are born. To produce and uphold these qualities of the energetic body or soul, it must necessarily have been, quite literally, "a state of innocence." At birth, these souls that have been dwelling in a state of emotional innocence and vulnerability are figuratively thrust out of the garden of innocence and into the dualistic world of love and violence, of honesty and deceit, of goodwill and malice.

Many qualities that objects possess or attributes that people demonstrate are considered to be part of a dualistic continuum, such as hot and cold, bitter and sweet, calm and anxious, loving and hateful. Each duality represents one complementary set of polar aspects. Each exists as a "compound-in-one,"[31] as neither half of any dualistic compound can exist without its complement. The degree to which a quality on either side of the dualistic continuum is distinguished is a direct result of the degree of contrast with its contrasting complement. For example, if someone has lived their entire life in a hot and dry climate with little seasonal variation and suddenly takes a trip to a cold and wet place, the individual will experience the aspects of "cold" and "wet" with a high degree of intensity due to the contrast with the climate that they have become accustomed to.

When people talk about "getting beyond dualism", they are necessarily referring to a state where there is no contrast or variance. Imagining such a state is easy to do: If all liquids were always kept at a lukewarm temperature, one would not experience the dual aspects of "hot" and "cold" in relationship to temperature of liquid as one would if alternating between iced and heated beverages. But the elimination of the dualistic variance and contrast actually eliminates the qualities by which temperature is experienced. All things that exist and are consciously experienced as objects, states, dynamics, or realities hold properties based upon the qualities and characteristics that these things possess or evoke. Qualities cannot be distinguished without variance, and therefore the elimination of variance between dual aspects removes also the qualities which allow for experience of an object, state, dynamic, or reality. The principle that realities exist and are known as complementary dualistic compounds-in-one is a premise that not only can be investigated and verified through sensory perception, but also aligns with scriptural description of the dualistic nature of this world:

> "For it must need be, that there is an opposition in all things... wherefore all things must needs be a compound in one; wherefore, if it should be as one body it must needs remain as dead, having no life neither death, nor corruption nor incorruption, happiness nor misery, neither sense nor insensibility."[32]

Whether one believes that the story of Adam and Eve is literal, symbolic, or a myth, innocent souls entering a realm where they acquire experiential knowledge of contrasting compliments makes the story of a fall from innocence intensely relevant for every human being.

Given that qualities can only be experienced where there is some degree of variance of that quality that can be distinguished, energetic bodies coming from any realm without energetic variance, such as a state of pure innocence and pure love, could by definition have no contrasting element whereby they could distinguish and know what these states of experience were. Had a transition into a dualistic realm not occurred, souls would necessarily have "remained in a state of innocence, having no joy, for they knew no misery" [33]. Once a soul enters into a duality, the variance of energetic quality births each soul into the capacity for distinguishing characteristics of its environment that were previously unknowable. Given the impossibility of experience without contrasting quality of it, the name given to the forbidden fruit being "of the tree of the knowledge of good and evil" [34] perfectly describes the result of partaking of it and the consequence of being thrust into a world of experiential knowledge in which many new realities could become "known". But the innocence that exists prior to entering these dualities is not something that can simply be stepped back into. For any soul to partake of "the tree of knowledge of good and evil"[35] literally or symbolically, would mean that in this act their innocence- in having not tasted of experience- would be broken; and they must necessarily be expelled from that state as they possess experiential "knowledge" that cannot be erased, nor the act repealed.

Had energetic bodies never left a state of singular energetic quality, it is true that they never would have entered into a world where they would have tasted corruption, but they would have not had a certain type of "knowledge" that the "Tree of the Knowledge of Good and Evil" gave them access to – experiential knowledge of all varieties. Therefore, to partake of the fruit would be a transgression of law by which states of energetic innocence could be maintained. Within the scriptural account of this transition, it is explained to Adam and Eve that if they partake of this fruit, then "your eyes shall be opened, and ye shall be as Gods...", in the possession of this new knowledge. [36] This knowledge opened up the possibility for negative and positive experience simultaneously, having opportunity "[t]o know the sweet having tasted the bitter" [37]. Therefore, transgression of the law brought many consequences, one of which had the potential for being something positive, the progression of the soul in an expanding of its capacities for experience. Whether taken literally or a as symbol to represent the transition of all souls into this dualistic world, by virtue of partaking of this fruit, Adam's transgression would open the possibility for spiritual progression.

BUILDING PRINCIPLES:

- There is opposition in everything, and it is not until one has experienced both sides of oppositional qualities that they become known to them.
- The scriptural story of the garden of Eden is one that has relevance for all souls, as there is evidence all have come from a plane of singular energetic quality into this realm of contrasting complements.

6

The Principle of Worth

DISEASE OF THE SOUL

In this world where love exists on a continuum with its polar opposite, souls often do not receive the substance of love in the quantity and quality needed to nurture their immortal body, and too often incur love's opposite. The infant's need for constant love, operating within an environment where love is often given conditionally or not at all, works to create a disease of fragility within the internal self. The infant's sense of personal worth, whether or not it is innately given, is initially affected by the expressions of these things that it receives from the external world. Where these expressions are given conditionally, the experience of being loved and valued becomes a conditional one. One moment, after being gently attended to, the self feels loved and strong; in the next, it may receive a message of harshness or disapproval sent either energetically or verbally and feel devalued. The experience of personal worth as conditional and externalized is shared by many in the human family.

In this chapter I want to acknowledge the ideas of John Powell, who in his books shares many insights into human nature, love as a human need, and a sense of personal worth as the product of love within a person. In one of his books, *The Secret of Staying in Love*, Powell gives a list of human actions stemming from a lack of love and sense of personal worth. I give a similar list in the second section of this chapter. The lists do have a few of the same human actions, many different, and all have different descriptions. But I want to acknowledge the influence of Powell's ideas on this chapter of the book.

As the soul is both energetically and intellectually conscious, the messages it absorbs regarding its worth and lovability are gleaned both from its energetic environment and through the images of itself derived from intellectual evaluations of experience. Conditional love, therefore, is felt energetically and understood conceptually, both avenues affecting aspects of the conscious and sentient energetic body. As feeling loved and of worth correlates to feeling joyful or depressed, fulfilled or empty, conditional lovability and worth translate directly into conditional peace and happiness. Where one's experience of worth and lovability is variable, the self is never satisfied. The moments of love and recognition from the outside world feel good when they come, but they are fleeting. The lack of a sense of inherent worth and lovability is an emptiness which seeks to be filled. But even much approval and success will not allow one to rest in a deep sense of peace and fulfillment, as the experience of conditional worth will only persist as long as all the external sources of worth and approval are upheld. The conditionally lovable self is never at rest, never at peace, as it must always work to control the outside world and ensure that the approval and success continue. Thus, being loved conditionally attacks the possibility of true inner peace, which requires the constancy of the experience of inherent personal worth and lovability.

The experience of feeling the absence of lovability and self-worth, even for a moment, is not pleasant; it is an experience that can be disconcerting, one of emptiness, anxiety, loneliness, insecurity, or disconnection. The absence of love in the energetic environment and environmental forces which are either nurturing or detrimental to the soul often leaves the energetic body in a state of energetic disease. This can take the form of physical illness and often includes various types of pain and discomfort. Similarly, the negative emotions are often more than psychological productions, but actually symptoms of spiritual disease manifesting as energetic unrest and discomfort. When people speak about finding peace, they are necessarily referring to a state where the energetic body is healthy. In the same manner that physical suffering and ailment is the pain of the physical body, fear, anxiety and every negative emotion are the pains of a diseased soul. Without understanding the nurturing and destructive forces in their energetic environment, yet desiring to eliminate the symptoms of spiritual pain and discomfort, human beings use a variety of methods to treat symptoms of spiritual disease:

COPING MECHANISMS

Overachieving/Perfectionism: One of the most common ways for a fragile self to protect against feeling any of these negative symptoms is to meet external conditions of worth so well that the individual will never be rejected for failure to do so. To the degree that a person has experienced success in trying to conform to external expectations, she will continue to try to do so. She has received approval as a reward for her conformity, and this reinforces the behavior. The quest to have more control over sources of validation turns into an endless attempt to conform to, and exceed, expectations. This dynamic is the root of perfectionism. In this way, by possession of qualities deemed praiseworthy by parents, teachers, and the greater culture, and by attempts at perfection of them, one secures as much as possible the persistence of approval from these sources.

In this case, the self compensates for its fragility with the pursuit of recognition, achievement, and perfectionism. Those who use this coping mechanism often try to impress people, try to find approval and exceed expectations, try to do, say, and be the things that will win the expression of love and worth from others. On a recent episode of "Now" on PBS, host David Brancaccio mentioned that the head of a respected business school recently said that he worries that since the people with the greatest drive are generally the ones with the least real self worth and the highest need to compensate for it through external accomplishments, the school is predominantly admitting and educating future societal leaders who neither love themselves nor are likely to run their business to really contribute to others. [1]

When perfectionism and overachievement are used as a protection of the self, and the individual wins recognition and approval for his level of performance, he becomes afraid ever to perform imperfectly or make a mistake. He is compelled always to perform at this high standard out of the fear that failure to do so will mean a loss of love and approval. Worth comes to ride so heavily on achievement and performance that even receiving a B paper can result in an experience of personal devastation. Sometimes, when someone has received an enormous amount of praise or recognition for a specific quality or trait – such as personal appearance, intelligence, or athletic ability – he or she comes to feel loved and considered valuable only for this trait. Such people feel that if they lost their beauty or talent, they would no longer be loved. Anorexia, for example, has a high correlation with externalized worth onto particular traits of one's physical body. Anorexics feel that they are unlovable if they do not fit an image of physical perfection they hold in their minds. They can therefore starve themselves of nutrition, and even risk killing themselves, because in their mind, the thing that gives them worth is their physical appearance or desirability and nothing else.

Attempts at Control: The attempt to control one's internal state, since it is connected to the external world and its approval, results in the attempt to control oneself, one's environment, the outcome of situations, and other people. Sometimes the attempt to control turns into the creation of rules and procedures one believes must be followed in order to ensure the best outcome. People who are extremely compliant rule followers or very rigidly follow their own sets of rules do so because such behavior provides a sense of security that these rules order their world and eliminate the possibility for things outside of their control to happen.

When excessive control is used as a coping mechanism, people will experience peace and fulfillment only so long as they are able to maintain the experience of control in their lives. When something happens that may jeopardize this ability to control, someone who has seemed very calm and ordered will suddenly demonstrate a great deal of fear, anxiety or anger. In reality, the potential of these symptoms was always present under the surface driving the force and desire to control.

Forms of Rationalization: In any event of failure to meet an external condition or expectation, rationalization works to create an internal defense against experiencing the symptoms of such failure. If one can come up with an explanation for how an undesirable outcome was inevitable, or was not one's own fault, one can avoid being personally accountable for mistakes and negative outcomes. One cannot be responsible for something that they had no accountability or cause over.

Placing blame is another form of rationalization born from the difficulty of the fragile self to bear responsibility for a mistake or undesirable set of circumstances. Therefore, when something goes wrong, one urgently searches for a place to pin the accountability, rationalizing to oneself and others that all undesirable features of oneself or one's life are the fault of others. If accountability for undesirable things is always placed elsewhere, one is protected from ever being accused of any mistake.

Playing the Victim: When a person is exhausted from trying to control things in the world to meet personal and external conditions and expectations, victimhood is a shelter which says, "I don't have control." Taking this perspective can ease the anxiety that goes along with attempting to control and failing, or it can simply become an excuse to avoid being held accountable. Victimhood can be a conscious or unconscious defense which turns the tables so that a person not only avoids accountability for his life, but might actually receive sympathy from others for it.

Distractions: When a person's internal state has any degree of unrest or discontent, shopping, television, video games, sexual preoccupation, exercise, and many other activities are often used to distract from this unrest. When people say "I always have to be doing something," they are describing the difficulty with being present with themselves and their experience naked of an activity or distraction to focus attention on.

Arrogance/Exaggerated Confidence: Acting superior or overly confident is a way to consciously convince oneself of one's worth in a situation where it is unconsciously fragile. If someone expresses grandiose confidence in herself or her abilities, or if a person must always claim her superiority or attempt to demonstrate it, often there is an unconscious feeling of inadequacy driving the need to continually demonstrate her worth.

Condemnation of oneself or others: People who do not love themselves may adapt to their condition by becoming critical of others, always finding and pointing out their faults. The activity of finding faults in others works as a distraction from noticing any faults within oneself. Self deprecation, on the other hand, is a proactive defensive against rejection and disapproval. When people self-deprecate, they often do so because they feel that if they tear themselves down, it will prevent others from desiring to do so. Self deprecation is also a way to evoke sympathy and consolation from friends and family who will then compliment and praise them and deny their self-insult.

***Energetic/Emotional Hardening* :** When the self is fragile, one of the most effective ways to avoid the pain of fluctuations of love from outside sources is to find ways to harden or numb one's ability to feel. When the energetic body has experienced harshness and rejection from others, it can learn to withdraw, numb, or harden itself so that it simply is not as affected by emotional rejection from others. In this hardening process one can use anger or indifference as a wall that shields anything from coming through from the outside. While energetic hardening keeps one from feeling the impact of the negative expressions of others, it also keeps out positive expressions of external sources.

Passivity or Domination: Through passively submitting oneself to the will of others, one who is sensitive to emotional rejection may avoid conflict. Domination, on the other hand, is a coping mechanism wherein people create situations in which they have the power to extend worth and approval to others or subject others to their demands. While it may seem, superficially, that someone who dominates other people is a very strong person, the compulsion and need to be always in a position of dominance over another demonstrates internal fragility, insufficient self worth to feel lovable in the absence of such relationships of power and importance.

Parent-child relationships are often vulnerable to dynamics of domination and passivity as children are in a position of inherent physical and practical dependency to parents. Where an individual has been subject to the domination of another at some point in their own life, children can become safe figures for a parent with an inclination to exert domination over another, in part due to their own past and forced submission or subservience. Given the imbalance of power in the parent-child relationship, the commonplace and culturally accepted practices of hitting children exacerbate this unhealthy human dynamic, but also have been proven to correlate to suppressed or increased overt aggression, and/ or energetic or emotional disconnection and hardening . In support of these findings, renowned Peditrician Dr. William Sears published an article entitled "10 reasons not to hit your child."[2]

These types of traumatic childhood events and their effects within the energetic body are noted by Barbara Brennan: "With HSP, you will be able to see a red haze around the angry person." [3] "To find out what is happening with her on a deeper level, it is possible to focus on the cause of the anger, not only in the present, but also how it relates to childhood experience and to her relationships with her parents. Under the red haze will appear a gray, thick, fluid-like substance that conveys a heavy sadness. By focusing on the essence of the gray substance, you will probably even be able to see the childhood scene that caused the deep rooted pain. You will see that the person habitually reacts in anger to certain situations, when perhaps crying is a more useful emotion to release ..."[4]

Defensiveness: Defensiveness is a psychological protection that arises when the fragile self feels that it has been attacked. The more easily a person feels attacked, or the more fragile his internal self really is, the more frequently and harshly he will become defensive when feeling emotionally threatened. In some cases, defensiveness actually gives way to pre-emptive attacks of other people, their behavior, or their perceptions, thus proactively demonstrating the superiority of one's own actions or positions even before they have even been challenged.

Isolation: Choosing to cut off relationships with people preemptively prevents the possibility of rejection within them. When one has experienced only conditional love, or felt injured in relationships, self-imposed isolation is an attempt to protect oneself from any further injury.

Substances: The most common methods of treatment of the spiritual disease of fragility of the Self, include a variety of substances and activities which attempt to affect one's quality of energetic experience. Yet ongoing contented or discontented energetic experience is ultimately a product of the health of the soul. When substances are used to produce an energetic or emotional effect, the change in experience will only be a temporary one. As the health of the soul is not addressed directly, since merely the symptom of its disease is treated, the disease and its symptoms of negative emotions will again become present when the effect of the substance has subsided.

Thus, the one-time use of a substance to produce an energetic effect quickly becomes a dependency on that substance to maintain that effect, and addiction is born. Addiction is caused by the energetic reliance on any substance or activity that will produce a desired effect in one's energetic body. People simply do not get addicted to things that do not affect their energy, and anything and everything that can affect the energetic body – sugar, food, caffeine, exercise, sex, drugs and alcohol – can become an energetic dependency. Such energetic dependencies, or "addictions," are considered to be negative in the following conditions:

1) If the substance or activity relied on is unhealthy in the quantity that one relies on it.
2) If, without this substance, one does not have the ability to feel energetically peaceful or healthy.
3) If the person is so energetically dependent that the drive to use the substance or perform the activity has more control over one's actions than one's mental willpower.

As the use of substances to artificially mask the negative effects of a diseased energetic body does nothing to heal the cause of the symptom, addiction can become a prison from which souls do not know how to escape. There is hope, however, for all people, no matter what state of dependency they are in. If the cause of the symptoms being treated is addressed directly by beginning to nurture the soul with positive thoughts, loving relationships, uplifting music, and the connection to the life of the soul, sources of spiritual light from the very home from which these energetic bodies first came, the energetic body will begin to heal, the pains of the diseased soul will find relief and the soul will experience more fully the fruits of spiritual health, even those of joy, and of peace. [5]

BUILDING PRINCIPLES:

- Personal sense of self-worth is just as important to the health of the soul as the environment it lives within.
- A general sense of peace and fulfillment represent spiritual health where negative emotions often represent the soul's request for energetic care. Symptoms of imperfect health within the energetic body are universal.
- Addressing the root cause of these symptoms through developing healthy relationships, and trying to connect with one's soul and sources of spiritual light increase its health and experience of joy, peace and fulfillment.

REMODELING EXERCISES:

- Are you happy with your spiritual or energetic sense of well-being?
- What are some of the things you do to positively affect your energetic state of experience, listen to music, exercise or do yoga, pray or meditate, etc.?

VULNERABILITY AND PROTECTION

After the entrance of souls into an energetic environment where the love that nurtures them exists amidst forces that harm them, many people in this world live with fragile and protected selves. From the list of coping mechanisms that arise where there is any deficiency in the experience of personal worth and lovability, one can make sense of just about every human behavior, with one notable exception. The exception to all these behaviors and attempts to make oneself feel greater internal worth and lovability is the act of loving. Loving is the only human activity which builds authentic worth and heals the disease of the fragile self; love, extended toward oneself and extended toward others, is the highest human endeavor.

The disease of the soul injures a person's ability to love as it creates tendency to protect oneself from others, which process of spiritual closing prohibits the possibility of giving and receiving love. One can only love when the self allows itself to be vulnerable and open. But the self cannot open when it is fragile and wounded; where the soul is in pain, it will close itself. People often wonder what happens to the innocent, carefree playfulness of childhood. Children are born sensitive to the expressions of love, contempt, and indifference of those around them. They express their emotions freely and openly. They do not censor themselves or suppress the desire to approach a potential playmate out of fear of rejection or criticism. As rejection or criticism of authentic self expression occurs, people begin to inhibit their expression to avoid the likelihood of such undesirable experiences in the future, and learn how to harden themselves emotionally so that if such rejection or criticism ever does come again, it will not be as painful.

An emotional wound does not always seem as real as a physical one, since it is not manifest on the surface of the skin, but the healing process may be much longer. While not every person experiences the same degree of emotional injury in their life, most people go through experiences which are emotionally painful and choose to become a little less sensitive in the future rather than continue to share the same level of vulnerability with others. In fact, many feel that it would be reckless not to do so, since the world and the temperaments of others one interacts with are unpredictable. The resultant world is one of people who are hardened to varying degrees and cannot feel fully compassionate towards each other because they have taken up armor to protect themselves emotionally.

Hardened hearts are what make conflict within the brother and sisterhood of humankind possible. This is the reason behind the scriptural passages that teach each person to become "as a little child" [6] who still maintains emotional softness toward others. A world of compassion is possible only with such childlike emotional vulnerability, as soft, unprotected hearts are more sensitive and maintain more sense of connection to other people and therefore cannot as easily do harsh things toward others. There is no other way to love another "as thyself " than to actually feel a sense of connection to others. Compassionate connection, or the ability "to suffer with" others, is impaired when people numb or protect themselves emotionally, because they don't feel "connected to" them. The ability for compassion requires first a sense of connection. Capacity to "suffer with" another is a function of how "connected to" other souls one has become.

The heart that has hardened itself in response to its energetic environment loses the ability to fully give and receive love. It is the greatest of all challenges to preserve emotional vulnerability on a plane of existence where such harshness of emotion exists, to continue to be loving in the face of aggression or insensitivity. Jesus' teaching to "love your enemies, do good to them which hate you, bless them that curse you, and pray for them which despitefully use you", [7] sounds radical at first. Yet every time a person chooses love rather than aggression or defensiveness, he helps the other to do the same. Every time that he responds to anger with anger or defense after being attacked, he will create even further hardness within the other as well as himself. When the British had rule of India, Gandhi advocated remaining non-violent even when aggressed against. He explained that in the moment they took a blow and did not retaliate, the other person's respect for them would increase, and their hatred of them would decrease.

Many people reading this section might say that becoming a mature adult, is a balance between vulnerability and protection, or having emotional defenses. Obviously, there are people and situations, that require caution, and more care then a child acting with openness and vulnerability. But the virtue of the principle that souls must "become like little children" becomes evident inside of the recognition that love is only possible where there is vulnerability. So recognizing where one is hardened to others, enables the possibility of change. To become as a child is to shed some of the emotional defenses and protections a person has garnered throughout his life, carefully, not recklessly. And there may certainly be a risk here on occasion. But it is a risk made for a worthy cause—love. And, as in the example of Gandhi's non-violence, the act of being loving is never wasted, maybe only in some cases of abusive relationships. Where the love one extends seems to be met with harshness or indifference, it will usually still work to change the other person, and make them kinder or less harsh in the future. That doesn't mean we can always be loving, just that it really is a worth while endeavor. It should be our goal wherever possible.

Living these principles, for each within his capacity to seek to become more vulnerable and loving, reverses the dynamic enacted due to the transition from a state of innocence into harsh duality – the resultant spiral of emotional injury and protection. By every loving, defenseless action one makes toward another, the spiral reverses: they help other souls to heal and to progress in their ability to love. Each individual has the power to love, the power to heal those injured by love's absence.

BUILDING PRINCIPLES:

- Love, given and received, heals spiritual injury at its source, dissolving the need for the coping mechanisms of spiritual disease.
- In order to combat harshness and injury in this world, one can choose to soften energetic protection in order to feel more connected to others.
- The principle of Love is the greatest building principle to include in a human structure of reality, as it seeks only to build oneself and others up. It never destroys or tears down.

7

The Principle of Purpose

THE LIFE REVIEW

Evidence expressed by those who have had near death experiences, consistent across all cultures of people and backgrounds of religion, is that the greatest thing of worth beyond this life concerns where one loves and fails to love others, that human worth and purpose revolves around the effect of our actions upon each other. [1] A common feature of the NDE in realms the experiencer travels to that are referred to as supernatural, is a "life review" performed in a dimension of reality where time is not experienced as linear:

> "Everything that had ever happened to me was simply there, in full view, contemporary and current, all seemingly taking place at that moment. How this was possible I didn't know. I had never before experienced the kind of space we seemed to be in…

There were other scenes, hundreds, thousands, all illuminated by the searing light, in an existence where time seemed to have ceased. It would have taken weeks of ordinary time even to glance at so many events, and yet I had no sense of minutes passing. [2]

The experience of the life review is one that is described as instilling incredible empathic concern for others. For the first time one not only experiences every emotion they maintained while living, but also those of persons with whom they interacted. They experience the effects of their actions upon others in a way that is not possible on the earth, literally having the very experiences and thoughts of every person that one's actions affected throughout mortality:

"Mine was not a review, but a reliving. For me it was a total reliving of every thought I had ever thought, every word I had ever spoken, and every deed I had ever done; plus the effect of each thought, word and deed on everyone and anyone who had come within my environment or sphere of influence whether I knew them or not... No detail was left out. No slip of the tongue or slur was missed. No mistake or accident went unaccounted for." [3]

"It seemed there would be no end to it. A vast number of those people I knew or had seen. Then there were hundreds I had never seen. These were people who had been indirectly injured by me. The minute history of my criminal career was thus relived by me, plus all the small injuries I had inflicted unconsciously by my thoughtless words and looks and omissions. Apparently nothing was omitted in this nightmare of injuries, but the most terrifying thing about it was that every pang of suffering I had caused others was now felt by me..."[4]

Most NDEers describe being in the experience of someone who they were mean or hurtful to as the single most transformative aspect of the experience. The literal definition of "compassion" is "to suffer with," not just to feel empathy, but to feel sorrow and pain at the sorrow and pain of another. As NDEers feel the sorrow and pain or the joy and happiness others feel as an effect of their own actions, they quite literally "suffer with" every other with whom they have ever directly or indirectly affected. Parents feel the broken hearts of their children when they repeatedly don't give time to them, or are harsh or insensitive. Having gone through what they describe as the most compassion evoking experience comprehensible, NDEers return to earth with a unique level of understanding of the way that we affect each other as human beings and the need to strive always to be compassionate.

The life review also gives a new perspective to the worth of one's actions. In day to day life all of the tangible aspects of success and security can become the priority over the state of one's heart and the way that one interacts with other human beings. Accounts of the life review demonstrate that the only things that are concrete in the life to come are those that are intangible in this one, the love and kindness that one imparts to those around them. This gives new meaning to the scriptural exhortation to "lay up for yourselves treasures in heaven, where neither moth nor rust doth corrupt, and where thieves do not break through nor steal", as kind and loving actions are tangible, recorded items of the world to come.[5]

The studies of psychological changes undergone in those who had near death experiences demonstrate the influence of being in this purely spiritual environment. The NDEr often no longer cares for wealth or status: "Before I was living for material things ... Before I was conscious of only me, what I had, what I wanted ... I have gradually sloughed off the desires to have and to hold earthly possessions, material possessions to any great degree." [6] Understanding fully the level to which our actions affect the well being of others – as the love or harshness we give literally affects the health of the souls with whom we interact – gives those who have had NDEs an understanding that the things of most worth ultimately are not things that we can hold in our hands. They are the impressions that each leaves on other souls, either for health or for detriment, over the course of life. Those who have near death experiences return to say that the quality of the relationships we maintain with family, friends, and others, and the impressions that we leave upon them are the primary material human beings can take from this life. [7]

> *Loving is the only human activity which builds authentic worth and heals the disease of the fragile self; love, extended toward oneself and extended toward others, is the highest human endeavor.*

The transformative power of the Near Death Experience in the life of the individual is that it awakens, or reawakens something within them.

Going through the life review and actually feeling the feeling of disappointment of one's child after ignoring them or the hurt of a spouse after being insensitive, awakens a deeper connection to the way in which we affect each other as human beings and how truly important our actions and treatment of each other actually is. It is a heart opening experience to feel the pain of another person, especially the pain that one caused themselves. Experientially knowing the capability of our actions to heal or cause injury works to reawaken their hearts. The state of our heart, and the love that we can give to others is the primary material human beings can take from this life. The joy and pain the soul experiences in the life review is in direct proportion to the love, indifference, or negativity that one has given to the lives of others. Every one of us will one day find ourselves in that same place being asked what we have done with our life. To know this and expect that upon death one's highest accountability will be how well one loved, is the opportunity to build one's structure of reality to include this principle. From the stories of many in that same place, it seems that this one principle may be of much greater weight in the end than many of the beams and walls that we took great care to erect.

BUILDING PRINCIPLES:

- Inside of relationships, all of our actions affect others, whether for spiritual health or detriment.
- Near Death Experiences teach that the things of most importance in the world to come are those that are intangible in this one- the effect of our actions upon other souls.

- The commitment to try and act always with love and kindness is, therefore, the single most important building material in this project.

REMODELING EXERCISES

- In reflecting on your relationships, is there any person to whom you could demonstrate appreciation, or express love, or do so more often?
- Is there any person that you know you have caused injury through your thoughts or actions that you could try and make amends, or ask for forgiveness?

PARABLE OF THE KING AND PRINCE

This world can feel permanent, with its day to day routine and established processes. Those who have almost lost their life, or who are given news that their time on this earth will soon be ending, are reawakened to the real priorities: spending time with friends and family, pursuing life dreams they may have set aside. The day to day routine concerns itself with many things that have nothing to do with our real purpose on this earth and can therefore become great distractions. In his book *What Are We Seeking*, TKV Desikachar relates a parable of our journey to this earth:

> "There is a story of a Prince who lived in a beautiful kingdom and who was sent by the King to search for a precious jewel in a land far away. The King explained that this was the tradition and an indispensable step for acquiring certain qualities

which could not be obtained otherwise. The Prince traveled to the land where the jewel was hidden, guarded by a fearsome monster. During the long journey he lost his royal appearance and a kind of sleep fell upon him. He forgot his mission. He became involved in the commercial life of this land and earned his living honorably and humbly. He was a respectable member of the community, acquiring riches and seeking to increase his wealth. But he had forgotten the task for which he had been sent. The King learned of his plight and, using a special power which was his alone, managed to awaken his son and remind him who he was and why he was there. The Prince developed a different way of looking at things, changed many of his attitudes and developed the clarity that later enabled him to find a method of sending the monster into a deep sleep. He took the jewel, rushed back to his father and realized the immense beauty of this real kingdom." [8]

In this analogy, all of us are likened to the Prince or Princess who is on a journey designed for our spiritual growth and development. Like the Prince, upon coming into this world, each of us has a veil placed over our remembrance of our true spiritual identity and purpose. We begin our life in the temporal world, and it feels so real that we believe our time and intentions should be spent on making our temporal existence the most secure, pleasurable, and rewarding one possible. These temporal pursuits can become all-consuming and keep each of us from discovering the mystery of our earthly mission. We were not sent here to be servants of the temporal world and its processes; the temporal world itself is here as a vehicle for our spiritual progression.

In this analogy, the journey to the jewel, or to defeat the monster, is likened to our unique purpose in this life. Finding love and a family might be the jewel, working against the monster of addiction, or pride or being a workaholic. Or the journey to the Jewel might be finding a path to serve others. The journey, and the nature of each individuals' spiritual purpose is unique. Like the King who uses the special power to awaken his son and remind him of who he was and why he was here, our spiritual parent has the ability to remind us of our true nature and purpose, to redirect us onto the path toward fulfillment of our missions while on this earth. These modes of communication and awakening can come in the form of a dream, personal intuition, a synchronistic experience, disease or illness, or a serious accident.

One of the dynamics of the day to day temporal routine is that it can become a rut that keeps us from looking up and remembering our true identity and purpose. In this mission, the King can call us back at any time, and we do not know the day or the hour when we may be called out of the temporal world. The challenge for the Prince or Princess is to prepare for this return and to live as much as possible, with an eye to the true mission and purpose for which he or she was sent. It is true that the Prince or Princess will have earthly responsibilities, but some of the challenge of conquering the monster is to be able to negotiate the temporal challenges that we face in such a way that we are best able to give intention to fulfillment of our true purpose. Even if we do not reach the monster or conquer him and locate the jewel that we make the journey to find, if we are called back to the King with diligent pursuit and clarity of our true mission, we will have received much of the benefit of the jewel, putting each on the path back to their spiritual home.

BUILDING PRINCIPLES:

- The structure of reality that you construct, and the principles you live by will be some of the determining factors in your life, and affect the spiritual character that you possess at the end of this life.
- It is easy to become caught up in activities in the material world and lose sight of spiritual purpose. The greatest challenge in living this earthly life is to find one's sense of purpose and return to the plane of spiritual light and purity from which all have come.

REMODELING EXERCISES:

- Are there any life dreams that you've set aside in just running the mechanics of life? What would it take to recover them?
- What are some of your highest priorities in life? Do feel you give enough time to them, and are there any less important things you can let go of to free up time for them.

ONE GREAT WHOLE

True and correct principles must, by definition, be in support of each other. Nothing that is true can conflict with anything else that is true. This book has sought to resolve the major areas of ideological discord between scientific and religious communities by providing scientifically measurable evidence of the existence and immortality of the human soul. Individually, evidence of the Human Energy Field, Near Death Experiences, or Birth Memories, are less powerful than considering all three together, as they all testify of the soul, but in different ways:

Evidence of the Human Energy Field supports understanding the soul as having a natural form and set of capacities, being affected for health or detriment by forces within its environment, and insomuch as it is tied to mental and emotional states of being, provides an explanation for all attempts to manipulate personal states of experience with activities, environments and substances. Evidence of Near Death Experience supports understanding of the soul's persistence beyond mortal death, and the true nature of its immortal identity and purpose. Evidence of birth memory supports understanding of the pre-mortal existence of the human soul, and the absolute purity of the realm it came from before entering this dualistic world.

While individually, any of these three areas support the truth of the existence of the human soul, taken together, they are stronger and provide a more complete picture of its nature and purpose. Integration of these principles pertaining to the soul with existing structures of human knowledge has revolutionary implications. It may not be long before instruments can provide an MRI type scan of the Human Energy Field, and diagnose precursors of cancer within the energetic body before they have taken root. The life dynamics creating energetic dysfunction will be distinguished and proactive measures taken to avoid disease, eventually decreasing reliance upon reactive methods of treating symptoms of disease. Perhaps the day will come when needing to proscribe pharmaceutical drugs will be seen as a failure and missing the formation of any disease before it manifests is unacceptable.

These principles provide opportunity to dissolve scientific and religious discord. Yet the immediate implication of accepting the truth of spiritual realities and evidences pertaining to them is that not all religious and spiritual doctrine about them is accurate. In attempting to complete a puzzle of the whole of all truth, the next logical step must be to consider accepted principles concerning spiritual realities within the context of these same evidences- the Human Energy Field, and NDEs. Ultimately, unity between Scientific and Religious understanding must drive unity between all religious and spiritual understanding; but finding unity and connection between Scientific and Religious understanding is the foundation, and the first step bringing all truth into One Great Whole.

> *For me it was a total reliving of every thought I had ever thought, every word I had ever spoken, and every deed I had ever done; plus the effect of each thought, word and deed on everyone and anyone who had come within my environment or sphere of influence whether I knew them or not...*

THE SEQUEL

The Spirit of God

Upon accepting the premise of the immortal identity of the human soul, there is an immediate urgency to understanding the nature of the world that it will move into upon mortal death and any spiritual laws that will affect its eternal welfare. This is certainly not a novel topic, but Near Death Experiences provide opportunity to examine theological premises taught by the world's religions in context of evidences relating to spiritual planes of existence. NDE case examples support the understanding that on the mountain of spiritual progression, like an actual mountain, there are paths that lead toward higher elevation and the soul's peace and joy in the eternal world, and others that lead toward deep chasms and an end to the progression of the soul in the world to come.

On this spiritual ascent, there are many who claim to have knowledge of the nature of the journey, the risks involved, and the precautions that will be necessary or required in order to reach the summit. The world's religions, spiritual paths and scriptural texts represent would be 'guides' and 'trailbooks' on this journey, yet teach conflicting principles. The sequel to One Great Whole explores these paths inside of Near Death evidences that relate to them, in an effort to determine which provide more accurate depictions of the eternal world. Ultimately, unity between Scientific and Religious understanding must drive unity between all religious and spiritual understanding; but finding unity and connection between Scientific and Religious understanding is the foundation, and the first step bringing all truth into One Great Whole.

References

CHAPTER 1:

1. Bible. Luke 11:17
2. Bible. John 8:32
3. Rollins, Peter. How (Not) to Speak of God. (Brewster, MA: Paraclete Press. 2006)

CHAPTER 2:

1. Brennan, Barbara Ann. Function of the Human Energy Field in the Dynamic Process of Health and Disease / Hands of Light. (New York, NY: Bantam Books, 1988) P. 20/ Hunt, Dr. Valorie, Massey, W., Weinberg, R., Bruyere, R., and Hahn, P., Project Report, a Study of Structural Integration of Neuromuscular, Energy Field, and Emotional Approaches. (U.C.L.A. , 1977). / Inyushin, V.M. On the Problem of Recording the Human Biofield. (Parapsychology in the USSR, Part II, San Francisco. Calif, Washington Research Ctr, 1981.)/ Experimental Measurements of the Human Energy Field. (New York: Energy Research Group 1973). / Kilner, Walter J. M.D. The Human Aura (Retitled and new edition of the Human Atmosphere. New Hyde Park, NY: University Books, 1965.)
2. Brennan, Barbara Ann. Hands of Light. (New York, NY: Bantam Books, 1988). P. 20
3. *Ibid*, P. 20
4. Talbot, Michael. The Holographic Universe. (Harper Collins.) 1991. P. 175
5. Ronald S. Miller, "Bridging the Gap: An Interview with Valerie Hunt," Science of Mind (October 1983) P.12
6. Kidson, Ruth. Acupuncture for Everyone: What It Is, Why It Works, and How It Can Help You (Healing Arts Press; Revised edition , 2000) / Hecker, Hans-Ulrich. Color Atlas of Acupuncture: Body

Points - Ear Points - Trigger Points (Complementary Medicine / Thieme, 2008). / Giovanni Maciocia CAc(Nanjing) The Foundations of Chinese Medicine: A Comprehensive Text for Acupuncturists and Herbalists. (Churchill Livingstone, 2005).
7. Ronald S. Miller, "Bridging the Gap: An Interview with Valerie Hunt," Science of Mind (October 1983) P.12
8. Schulz, Mona Lisa. Awakening Intuition. (New York, NY: Three Rivers Press, 1999) Brennan, Barbara Ann. Hands of Light. (New York, NY: Bantam Books, 1988) PP. 3-4
9. *Ibid*, PP. 3-4
10. Talbot, Michael. The Holographic Universe. (Harper Collins.) 1991. P. 175
11. Utts, Jessica. "An Assessment of the evidence for psychic functioning." Prepared for the U.S. Central Intelligence Agency through the American Institute of Research, Division of Statistics, University of California, Davis, 1995.
12. Targ, Russel & Katra, Jane. Miracles of Mind. (Novato, CA: New World Library. 1999) PP. 35-36
13. *Ibid*, P. 7
14. Talbot, Michael. The Holographic Universe. (Harper Collins.) 1991. P. 192
15. Raymond Moody. Life After Life. (Mockingbird Books 1975)The Association for Near Death Studies, Inc. Durham, NC/ www.iands.org
16. Talbot, Michael. The Holographic Universe. (Harper Collins.) 1991. P. 242
17. Raymond Moody. Life After Life. (Mockingbird Books 1975) P.15
18. Talbot, Michael. The Holographic Universe. (Harper Collins.) 1991. P. 242-243
19. *Ibid*, P. 242-243. Morse, Melvin. Where God Lives. (New York, NY: First Cliff Street Books. 2001.)
20. *Ibid*, P. 242-243/ Morse, Melvin. Where God Lives. (New York, NY: First Cliff Street Books. 2001.).
21. Morse, Melvin. Where God Lives. (New York, NY: First Cliff Street Books. 2001. P.4) Moody, Raymond A. Jr. with Paul Perry, The Light Beyond (New York, NY: Bantam Books, 1988) PP.14-15
22. Talbot, Michael. The Holographic Universe. (Harper Collins.) 1991. P. 241
23. Raymond Moody. Life After Life. (Mockingbird Books 1975) P. 11-15
24. *Ibid*, P. 8
25. *Ibid*, P 27-28
26. *Ibid*, P. 28-29
27. Talbot, Michael. The Holographic Universe. (Harper Collins.) 1991. P. 242
28. *Ibid*, P. 167
29. *Ibid*, P. 245

30. *Ibid*, P. 245
31. *Ibid*, P. 245
32. National Cancer Institute.
33. De La Warr, G. Matter in the Making. (London : Vincent Stuart, 1996) / Brennan, Barbara Ann. Hands of Light. (New York, NY: Bantam Books, 1988) P. 31, 150-151.
34. Talbot, Michael. The Holographic Universe. (Harper Collins.) 1991. PP. 167-168 / Brennan, Barbara Ann. Hands of Light. (New York, NY: Bantam Books, 1988)
35. *Ibid*, PP. 7-69
36. Emoto, Masuro. The Hidden Massages in Water. (Hillsboro, OR: Beyond Words Publishing, Inc. 2001.)/ Emoto, Masuro. Love Thyself - The Message from Water III. (Carlsbad, CA: Hay House. 2004.)
37. Morse, Melivin. Where God Lives. (New York, NY: First Cliff Street Books. 2001.)
38. The Association for Near Death Studies, Inc. Durham, NC/ www.iands.org
39. *Ibid*
40. *Ibid*
41. Hegerty, Barbara Bradley. Fingerprints of God: The Search for the Science of Spirituality. (England: Riverhead Books, 2009)

CHAPTER 3:

1. Talbot, Michael. The Holographic Universe. (Harper Collins.) 1991. P.41
2. *Ibid*, P. 41
3. David Bohm, "Hidden Variables and the Implicate Order," in Quantum Implications, ed. Basic J. Jiley and F. David Peat. (London: Routledge & Kegan Pual, 1987) P. 38
4. Talbot, Michael. The Holographic Universe. (Harper Collins.) 1991. P. 49
5. *Ibid*, P. 168 / Brennan, Barbara Ann. Hands of Light. (New York, NY: Bantam Books, 1988).
6. Lipton, Bruce. The Biology of Belief. (Santa Rosa, CA: Elite Books. 2005) P. 9
7. *Ibid*, P. 30

CHAPTER 4:

1. Lipton, Bruce. The Biology of Belief. (Santa Rosa, CA: Elite Books. 2005) P. 16, 23
2. Talbot, Michael. The Holographic Universe. (Harper Collins.) 1991. Talbot. P. 192
3. Hegerty, Barbara Bradley. Fingerprints of God: The Search for the Science of Spirituality. (England: Riverhead Books, 2009)
4. Lipton, Bruce. The Biology of Belief. (Santa Rosa, CA: Elite Books. 2005) P. 16
5. *Ibid*, P. 16
6. *Ibid*, P. 15
7. *Ibid*, P. 26
8. *Ibid*, P. 26
9. *Ibid*, P. 29
10. *Ibid*, P. 38
11. Bible. Luke 20:19
12. Emoto, Masuro. The Hidden Massages in Water. (Hillsboro, OR: Beyond Words Publishing, Inc. 2001.) P. 51
13. *Ibid*, P. 51
14. Ohio State University Medical Center
15. Brennan, Barbara Ann. Hands of Light. (New York, NY: Bantam Books, 1988). P. 20
16. William Tiller Foundation/ Brennan, Barbara Ann. Hands of Light. (New York, NY: Bantam Books, 1988). P. 20
17. Ravitz, L. J. Bioelectric Correlates of Emotional States. (Conn State Medical Journal, 1952, Vol 16, pp 499-505. / Daily Variations of Standing Potential Differences in Human Subjects. (Yale Journal of Biology and Medicine, 1951, Vol 24, pp. 22-25.)
18. Bible. Proverbs 23:7
19. Brennan, Barbara Ann. Hands of Light. (New York, NY: Bantam Books, 1988)./ Schulz, Mona Lisa. Awakening Intuition. (New York, NY: Three Rivers Press, 1999)

CHAPTER 5:

1. Powell, John. The Secret of Staying in Love. Thomas Moore Publishing. 1974. P. 8
2. *Ibid*, P. 22
3. *Ibid*, P. 22
4. *Ibid*, P. 7/ Erich Fromm. Escape from Freedom. Henry Holt and Company. New York, NY. 1965
5. Bible. Matt 22:39
6. Powell, John. The Secret of Staying in Love. Thomas Moore Publishing. 1974. P. 9

REFERENCES

7. Verny, Thomas. The Secret Life of the Unborn Child. Dell Publishing. New York, NY. 1981. P. 65
8. *Ibid*, P. 65
9. Sarah J. Buckley. "Lotus Birth- A Ritual for our times". In the E-Book- Gentle Birth, Gentle Mothering, 2005.
10. Yao AC, Lind J. Effect of gravity on placental transfusion. *Lancet*, 1969, PP. 505-8. / Yao AC, Lind J. Placental transfusion. *Am J Dis Child*, 1974, 127:128-141./ Peltonen T. Placental transfusion advantage and disadvantage. *Eur J Pediatr*, 1981, 137:141-146 / Linderkamp O. Placental transfusion: determinants and effects. *Clin Perinatol*, 1982, 9:559-593.
11. Elizabeth Pantley. The No Cry Sleep Solution. (New York, NY: McGraw Hill. 2002) P. 4
12. Verny, Thomas. The Secret Life of the Unborn Child. Dell Publishing. New York, NY. P. 66
13. Bible. Jeremiah 1:5
14. Chamberlain, David. Babies Remember Birth. Jeremy T. Parcher, Inc. Los Angeles, Ca. 1988. Distributed by St. Martin's Press. New York. P. 186
15. *Ibid*, P. 188
16. *Ibid*, P. 187
17. *Ibid*, P. 191
18. *Ibid*, P. 157
19. Bible. Jeremiah 1:5
20. Ritchie, George. Return from Tomorrow. P. 64
21. Chamberlain, David. Babies Remember Birth. Jeremy T. Parcher, Inc. Los Angeles, Ca. 1988. Distributed by St. Martin's Press. New York P. 147
22. *Ibid*, P. 143
23. *Ibid*, P. 99
24. *Ibid*, P. 101
25. *Ibid*, P. 103
26. *Ibid*, P. 103
27. *Ibid*, PP. 103-104
28. *Ibid*, P. 186
29. *Ibid*, P. 186
30. Talbot, Michael. The Holographic Universe. (Harper Collins.) 1991. PP. 167-168 / Brennan, Barbara Ann. Hands of Light. (New York, NY: Bantam Books, 1988)
31. Book of Mormon. 2 Nephi 2:11
32. *Ibid*
33. *Ibid*, Nephi 2:23
34. Bible. Genesis 2:9 / 2:27
35. *Ibid*
36. Bible. Genesis 3:5
37. Doctrine & Covenants. Section 29:39

CHAPTER 6:

1. http://www.pbs.org/now/
2. William Search. 10 Reasons not to hit your child. (www.askdrsears.com).
3. Brennan, Barbara Ann. Hands of Light. (New York, NY: Bantam Books, 1988)
4. Brennan, Barbara Ann. Hands of Light. (New York, NY: Bantam Books, 1988)
5. Powell, John. The Secret of Staying in Love. Thomas Moore Publishing. 1974.
6. Bible. Mark 10:15, Luke 18:17
7. Bible. Matt 5:44

CHAPTER 7:

1. Bailey/ Ring/ IANDS
2. Ritchie. P. 49
3. P.M.H. Atwater. Coming Back P. 36
4. David Lorimer. Whole in One. P. 23
5. Bible. Matt 6:20
6. Ring. P. 132/ Bailey. P. 376/ The Association for Near Death Studies, Inc. Durham, NC
7. Bailey/ Ring/ IANDS
8. Desikachar, T.K.V. "What Are We Seeking". (India: Krishnamacharya Yoga Mandiram. 2002)

NOTES ON REFERENCES:

1. Biblical references are all taken from the King James Version of the Bible.

2. D & C is the abbreviation for Doctrine and Covenants.

www.ingramcontent.com/pod-product-compliance
Lightning Source LLC
Chambersburg PA
CBHW071406290426
44108CB00014B/1703